SAMUEL JOHNSON

The Latin Poems

SAMUEL JOHNSON

The Latin Poems

Translated and Edited
by Niall Rudd

Lewisburg
Bucknell University Press

Associated University Presses
2010 Eastpark Boulevard
Cranbury, NJ 08512

The paper used in this publication meets the requirements of the American National Standard for Permanence of Paper for Printed Library Materials Z39.48–1984.

Library of Congress Cataloging-in-Publication Data

Johnson, Samuel, 1709–1784.
[Poems. English & Latin. Selections]
The Latin poems / translated and edited by Niall Rudd.
p. cm.
Poems in Latin with English translations and commentary.
Includes bibliographical references and index.
ISBN 0-8387-5612-3 (alk. paper)
1. Johnson, Samuel, 1709–1784—Translations into English. 2. Latin poetry, Medieval and modern—England—Translations into English. I. Rudd, Niall. II. Title.

PA8540.J63A24 2005
821′.6—dc22

2004029079

PRINTED IN THE UNITED STATES OF AMERICA

Contents

Preface

THE AIMS OF THIS BOOK ARE LIMITED:

1. To provide a more accurate text of the poems. The standard text, as represented by Yale (1964) and Oxford (1974), turned out to be faulty in a surprising number of places. Departures from Yale and Oxford are indicated by italics, which are easily distinguishable from italicized proper names.

2. To offer a fairly literal translation that would enable the reader with rusty or even residual Latin to follow the originals. Oxford gives no translation; Yale's verse translations are of little help, and in the case of Johnson's epigrams from the *Greek Anthology,* instead of a translation, the reader has to make do with the Loeb version of the Greek. David Venturo (1999), in addition to a sympathetic literary study in chapter 5, gives a generous selection, but the translations are not always close. In Barry Baldwin's pioneering book (1995), the versions, though frequently elegant and idiomatic, are occasionally incorrect. He has also, for reasons of space, omitted translations when the English original is available, as in the case of Pope's *Messiah,* with the result that the reader is not in a position to see how Johnson has handled his model. Except for *Postgenitis* (O.85–7), where Johnson's own version is printed, and the lines on Pope's grotto (O.93), which stick quite closely to the original, I have supplied translations.

3. To explain possible obscurities in the poems and to provide occasional comments on their style. I have also included the more relevant classical allusions.There may well be further allusions to works in neo-Latin like those listed by David Money (2002). I am sadly ignorant in that field, but quotations in the prose literature of the eighteenth century would suggest that in Johnson's poems too the classical writers predominate. Horace turns out to be the most frequent source, no doubt because he was not only a clubbable man who commented memorably on life and people, but also a brilliant versifier in several metres. It is worth adding that Horace, too, was no stranger to depression; so one should not be surprised to see him in the background of some of Johnson's most somber poems.

For ease of reference I have followed Oxford's sequence, even where the chronology may be open to question. I have little to say on matters of history and provenance; abundant information may be found in the Yale and Oxford editions, and more recently in Baldwin's book, which contains interesting discussions and many independent suggestions. For other material the reader is referred to the bibliography, compiled with the kindly assistance of Professor Greg Clingham.

It remains to record my thanks to the late Professor W. S. Watt and Professor R. G. M. Nisbet, with whom I discussed a number of textual problems; their own suggestions are recorded in the notes. I am also grateful to the anonymous reader, whose learning and vigilance improved my original version and saved me from some careless errors. Mr. Scott Gibson helped in the preparation of the typescript. The Latin text is based on *The Poems of Samuel Johnson,* 2nd edition, edited by D. Nichol Smith and E. L. McAdam (1974), with the kind permission of the Oxford University Press.

Introduction

THIS WORK IS BASED ON A SIMPLE PREMISE: NAMELY, THAT IN THE CASE of a major figure like Johnson the reader should have access to all his work. Johnson himself would not have wished that, in an age when very few can read the language, his Latin poetry should be consigned to a separate category, closed to most educated people. The range of the poems is considerable. The epigrams from the *Greek Anthology* were, at least initially, composed at night during bouts of insomnia, even if they were revised and polished later. These pieces represent a wide variety of topics, and display not only Johnson's dexterity as a versifier but also occasionally his willingness to give the epigrams a new thrust toward moralizing or satire. They themselves have no religious content; they served rather to distract the writer from more serious thoughts. Much earlier, his lighthearted occasional poems had started with pieces like the complaint about college beer (O.40), and then continued with the flattery of Elizabeth Carter (58), a satirical squib against Walpole's government (85), and the teasing of Crisp over his liking for the theatre (180). A deeper note is struck in the verses on Skye and Inchkenneth. The first ode on Skye (193) turns into a reflection on peace of mind, the second (194–95) ends with affectionate thoughts of Mrs. Thrale, and the poem on Inchkenneth (196) celebrates the virtuous and cultivated lifestyle of Sir Alan McLean and his family. Different kinds of tribute are paid to Pope (45–49, 93), to the publisher Cave (55–56), to Dr. Lawrence (231–32), and, more generally, to the Christian way of life (237–38). The most striking passages, however, come in the middle of "Know Yourself" (188–89, vv. 24–41), a dreadful description of a mind on the verge of collapse, in the charming recollections of swimming as a boy in the stream at Stowe Mill (261), and in the anguished appeals for mercy in the devotional poems (e.g., 238–40, 266), which convert some of the Church's collects into deeply personal prayers. It has often been noted that the Latin form seems to have enabled Johnson to reveal things about himself that he would not have expressed in English. At the same time, in offering up these prayers Johnson was joining the great host of the faithful, who for seventeen centuries had drawn comfort from the Christian message.

The Latin poems supplement at several points our knowledge of the author. Thus the piece on the stream at Stowe Mill just mentioned adds to the little that is known about Johnson's childhood at Lichfield; "Know Thyself" vividly describes Johnson's feelings about his labors on the *Dictionary.* This piece links up with tributes like that in the diploma of the Dublin doctorate (1765—ten years before Oxford's), which was awarded "ob egregiam scriptorum elegantiam et utilitatem" (Hill and Powell 1934, 1.489), where the *utilitas* is clearly an allusion to the *Dictionary;* that same poem is also connected with Boswell's reference to the "morbid melancholy" that was lurking in Johnson's constitution (1.63). The feelings expressed in the piece addressed to Dr. Lawrence (231–32) are movingly elaborated in the passage ending "a friend whom long familiarity has much endeared. Lawrence is one of the best men whom I have known" (4.143), and in the Latin prose letter that follows, ending "postquam tu discesseris, quo me vertam?" [Once you have departed, where shall I turn?]. The "Prayer on Losing the Power of Speech" (237) provides a vivid illustration of Johnson's letter to Mrs. Thrale of June 19, 1783 (4.229–31). His affection for the same lady (*Oda* 194–95) is shown to be reciprocated in *Life* 2.427, where she says to Boswell "You and I *love* him." And, in a lighter vein, the "Motto for a Goat" (183) and the translation of Oldys's poem on the fly (197–98) remind us of Johnson's regard for his cat, Hodge, for whom he bought oysters, and his haste to make amends when he perceived that Hodge was "out of countenance" (4.197).

All these observations show that in Doctor Johnson's case complaints about "the biographical fallacy" are at their most irrelevant. While Shakespeare stands at one end of the spectrum, being both everyone and no one ("Others abide our question. Thou art free"), Johnson stands at the other. Although, as Boswell admits, only a small selection of his sayings and doings have been recorded, he is immediately recognizable as "one of us"—though built on a larger scale with heightened characteristics. Whether dominating the dinner-table conversation with his wit and wisdom, or lying awake in pain, dreading the last judgment, he remains an unforgettable personality, one who enlarges our conception of what it means to be human.

Abbreviations

O *The Poems of Samuel Johnson.* Edited by D. Nichol Smith and E. L. McAdam, Jr. 2nd edition. Oxford: Clarendon Press, 1974.

Y *Samuel Johnson.* Poems. Edited by E. L. McAdam, Jr., with George Milne. New Haven: Yale University Press, 1964.

B *The Latin and Greek Poems of Samuel Johnson: Text, Translation, and Commentary.* Edited by Barry Baldwin. London: Duckworth, 1995.

SAMUEL JOHNSON

The Latin Poems

1
Early Poems

O.40, Y.75, B.54 This piece was improvised jointly by Johnson and Dr. James; O assigns it to the late 1720s or early 1730s. For discussion see B.54–57.

Ad Lauram Parituram Epigramma

(An Epigram to Laura When About to Give Birth)

Angliacas inter pulcherrima, Laura, puellas,
  Mox uteri pondus depositura grave,
Adsit, Laura, tibi facilis Lucina dolenti;
  Neve tibi noceat praenituisse Deae.

Laura, most beautiful among the girls of England, soon to lay down the heavy burden of your womb, may Lucina be present, Laura, giving ease to your pain, and may it do you no harm that you outshone the Goddess.

This, and the next few poems, are written in elegiac couplets; i.e., a hexameter followed by a pentameter: the scheme is:

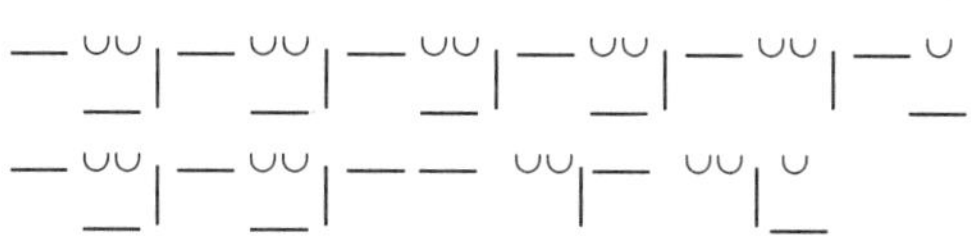

3. *Lucina:* the goddess of childbirth, usually identified with Juno or Diana. **4.** *Praenitere* is used in a context of amatory jealousy in Horace, *Odes* 1.33.4.

O.40, Y.27, B.9 The next two items were written when Johnson was at school or college.

Mea Nec Falernae etc.

Quid mirum Maro quod digne canit "Arma virumque"?
  Quid quod putidulum nostra Camoena sonat?
Limosum nobis promus dat callidus haustum,
  Virgilio vires uva Falerna dedit.
Carmina vis nostri scribant meliora poetae?
  Ingenium iubeas purior haustus alat.

What wonder that Maro sings worthily of "Arms and the man"? What wonder that our Muse sounds a bit rotten? The cunning steward gives us a muddy drink; the Falernian grape gave Virgil his power. Do you want our poets to write better songs? Order a purer draught to nourish their talent.

Title: from Horace, *Odes* 1.20.10–12 "mea nec Falernae / temperant vites neque Formiani / pocula colles" (My cups are not mellowed by Falernian vines or Formian hills). Maecenas is warned that when he visits Horace he will not be offered any of the high-class vintages that come from the area in the south of Latium and northern Campania. Johnson's logic should not be pressed too hard; for Horace managed to write quite well on his cheap drink.

1. Virgil's full name was Publius Vergilius Maro.

O.41, Y.28, B.17

Adjecere Bonae etc.

Quas Natura dedit dotes, Academia promit,
  Dat menti propriis Musa nitere bonis.
Materiam statuae sic praebet marmora Tellus,
  Saxea Phidiaca spirat imago manu.

The gifts conferred by Nature are developed by the University; the Muse allows the mind to shine by its own qualities; similarly Earth provides the statue's material—marble; but the stony image receives the breath of life thanks to the hand of Phidias.

Title: from Horace, *Epist.*2.2.43, "adiecere bonae paulo plus artis Athenae," where the poet speaks of the Academy at Athens adding a little more training to his education (*bonae* probably refers to *Athenae* rather than to *artis*). The training in question is then said to be in moral philosophy. For Horace *ars* is often regarded as a training which develops a person's inborn *ingenium;* thus the Muses' gift was *ingenium* (e.g., *Ars Poetica* 83, 323–24); its potential was fulfilled by the mind's other abilities (practice, self-criticism etc.). That, I take it, is what Johnson means in v. 2. The analogy in vv. 3–4, however, where the natural material of marble is worked into a lifelike statue, is not wholly clear; for Phidias's contribution is itself a combination of *ingenium* and *ars.* Horace's typically sensible position is summed up in *Ars Poetica,* 408–11, "Is it a gift (*natura*) or a craft (*ars*) that makes outstanding poetry? / I fail, myself, to see the good either of study (*studium*) / without a spark of genius (*sine divite vena*) or of untutored talent (*rude ingenium*). / Each requires the other's help in a common cause"; there is an ethical analogy in *Odes* 4.4.33: "doctrina . . . vim promovet insitam" (Training develops inborn powers).

4. Phidias (active c. 465–425 BC) was one of the greatest of the Greek sculptors.

O.41–2,Y.28, B.19 A school or undergraduate exercise.

Aurora Est Musis Amica

Cum caput Hesperiis attollit Phoebus ab undis,
  Atque Aethra ambigua pallida luce rubet,
Harmonia tellus completur lata, per agros
  Curas mulcentes dulce queruntur aves.
Rorem, qui segetes geniali et gramina succo
  Nutrit mane, putes esse Heliconis aqua;
Tunc vati facilem se praebet Apollo, Sibyllae
  Vix majore Deus corda furore quatit.
Carmine praebentur bellantia numina digne,
  Assurgitque epicis pagina docta modis.
Hinc annis panguntur delenda poemata nullis
  Queis majus pretium saecula lapsa dabunt.
Quid mirum? cum saxa movet statuasque tacentes
  Ignis quem Phoebi naribus efflat equus,

Quos pulsata sonos edit lyra pollice, primis
Percussa a radiis Memnonis ora dabant.

Dawn is a Friend to the Muses

When Phoebus raises his head from the Hesperian waves, and pale Aethra grows red with faint light, the broad earth is filled with harmony, throughout the countryside the birds make sweet complaints soothing (men's) cares. You would think that the dew which nourishes the crops and grass in the early morning with its cheering juice was from the water of Helicon. Then Apollo reveals himself readily to the poet; scarcely greater is the frenzy with which the God shakes the Sibyl's heart. In verse warring deities are worthily presented, and the learned page rises in epic strains; through the same force songs are composed which no number of years will destroy—songs to which the passing ages will give ever greater value. What wonder, when the fire breathed from the nostrils of Phoebus's horse moves rocks and silent statues, and the mouth of Memnon, when struck by his first rays, would give forth sounds which the lyre produces when struck by the thumb?

1. The young composer has carelessly put "Western" instead of "Eastern." **6.** *aquam* would be more correct Latin; but *aqua* is what Johnson wrote. The water of Mt. Helicon in Boeotia comes from the spring of Hippocrene. **7–8.** Johnson wrongly spells her name *Sybillae*—a common error. The context is Virgil, *Aen.* 6.46–51 and 77–80, where Apollo takes possession of his priestess. **11.** The line has a syllable too many; see Rudd (2000, 216–17). **14.** Phoebus Apollo is the sun god. **15–16.** The broken statue of Amenophis III at Thebes in Upper Egypt gave out a musical note when the stones were heated by the rising sun (Mayor 1888, 2.359–60); hence the statue was called "Memnon," who in Greek mythology was the son of Aurora, the dawn. *Percussa* is Wimsatt's convincing restoration of the damaged original.

O.43, Y.29, B.23 Also composed at Oxford.

A Translation of Dryden's Epigram on Milton

Dryden's piece went as follows:
Three poets, in three distant ages born,
Greece, Italy and England did adorn.

The first in loftiness of thought surpass'd,
The next in majesty, in both the last:
The force of Nature could no farther go;
To make a third, she join'd the former two.

Johnson translates thus:

Quos laudet vates Graius, Romanus et Anglus
  Tres tria temporibus secla dedere suis.
Sublime ingenium Graius; Romanus habebat
  Carmen grande sonans; Anglus utrumque tulit.
Nil majus Natura capit: clarare priores
  Quae potuere duos tertius unus habet.

Three ages gave to their times three poets whom Greek, Roman, and Englishman could praise. The Greek (poet) had a sublime mind, the Roman an impressively sonorous poem, the English exhibited both. Nature can produce nothing greater: the third on his own has the qualities that succeeded in making the first two famous.

1–2. Dryden shows that this is the meaning of "Graius, Romanus et Anglus." **3–4.** Here, however, Johnson uses the same three words to refer to Homer, Virgil, and Milton. The result is confusing. Dryden's basic idea, though neat in principle, could not be convincingly worked out. For while Homer's "rapidity" could have been set against Virgil's "stateliness," "rapidity" was not a feature of Milton. Homer's "loftiness of thought," on the other hand, was too close to Virgil's "majesty." Johnson tried to establish a more intelligible antithesis by interpreting 'majesty' in terms of sound, but he finished by setting a type of *ingenium* (i.e., an inner quality) against a type of *carmen.* For these reasons Cowper's version is superior:

Tres tria, sed longe distantia, saecula vates
  Ostentant tribus e gentibus eximios.
Graecia sublimem, cum maiestate disertum
  Roma tulit, felix Anglia utrique parem.
Partibus ex binis Natura exhausta coacta est,
  Tertius ut fieret, consociare duos.

Three ages, far distant in time, display three outstanding poets from three nations. Greece brought forth a sublime one, Rome one majestic in his eloquence, happy England one who was equal to each. Exhausted by two births, Nature was obliged to combine the two that the third might come into being.

O.45–49, Y.30–33, B.26–8

Pope's Messiah

This poem, an imitation of Virgil's fourth Eclogue (foretelling the birth of a marvelous child who would bring peace to the world), incorporates several passages of Isaiah. Many of the passages were noted by Pope himself. The poem was printed in *The Spectator* of May 14, 1712. Johnson's version belongs to December 1728.

Ye Nymphs of *Solyma!* begin the Song:
To heav'nly Themes sublimer Strains belong.
The Mossie Fountains and the Sylvan Shades,
The Dreams of *Pindus* and th'*Aonian Maids,*
Delight no more—O thou my Voice inspire
Who touch'd *Isaiah*'s hallow'd Lips with Fire!
Rapt into future Times, the Bard begun:
A *Virgin* shall conceive, a *Virgin* bear a Son!
From *Jesse*'s Root behold a Branch arise,
Whose sacred Flow'r with Fragrance fills the Skies.
Th' Aetherial Spirit o'er its Leaves shall move,
And on its Top descends the Mystic Dove.
Ye Heav'ns! from high the dewy Nectar pour,
And in soft Silence shed the kindly Show'r!
The Sick and Weak the healing Plant shall aid,
From Storms a Shelter, and from Heat a Shade.
All Crimes shall cease, and ancient Fraud shall fail;
Returning Justice lift aloft her Scale;
Peace o'er the World her Olive-Wand extend,
And white-roab'd Innocence from Heav'n descend.
Swift fly the Years, and rise th' expected Morn!
Oh spring to Light, auspicious Babe be born!
See Nature hasts her earliest Wreaths to bring,
With all the Incence of the breathing Spring:
See lofty *Lebanon* his Head advance,
See nodding Forests on the Mountains dance;
See spicy Clouds from lowly *Saron* rise,
And *Carmel's* flow'ry Top perfumes the Skies!
Hark! a glad Voice the lonely Desert chears;
Prepare the Way! a God, a God appears;
A God, a God! the vocal Hills reply,

The Rocks proclaim th' approaching Deity.
Lo, Earth receives him from the bending Skies!
Sink down ye Mountains, and ye Vallies rise:
With Heads declin'd, ye Cedars, Homage pay;
Be smooth ye Rocks, ye rapid Floods give Way!
The SAVIOR comes! by ancient Bards foretold;
Hear him ye Deaf, and all ye Blind behold!
He from thick Films shall purge the visual Ray,
And on the sightless Eye-ball pour the Day.
'Tis he th' obstructed Paths of Sound shall clear,
And bid new Musick charm th' unfolding Ear.
The Dumb shall sing, the Lame his crutch foregoe,
And leap exulting like the bounding Roe.
No Sigh, no Murmur the wide World shall hear,
From ev'ry Face he wipes off ev'ry Tear.
In Adamantine chains shall Death be bound,
And Hell's grim Tyrant feel th' eternal Wound.
As the good Shepherd tends his fleecy Care,
Seeks freshest Pasture and the purest Air,
Explores the lost, the wand'ring Sheep directs,
By Day o'ersees them, and by Night protects;
The tender Lambs he raises in his Arms,
Feeds from his Hand, and in his Bosom warms:
Thus shall Mankind his Guardian Care ingage,
The promis'd Father of the future Age.
No more shall Nation against Nation rise,
Nor ardent Warriors meet with hateful Eyes,
Nor Fields with gleaming Steel be cover'd o'er,
The Brazen Trumpets kindle Rage no more;
But useless Lances into Scythes shall bend,
And the broad Faulchion in a Plow-share end.
Then Palaces shall rise; the joyful Son
Shall finish what his short-liv'd Sire begun;
Their Vines a Shadow to their Race shall yield,
And the same Hand that sow'd shall reap the Field.
The Swain in barren Deserts with surprize
Sees Lillies spring, and sudden Verdure rise,
And starts amidst the thirsty Wilds to hear
New Falls of Water murm'ring in his Ear:
On rifted Rocks, the Dragon's late Abodes,
The green Reed trembles, and the Bulrush nods.

Waste sandy Vallies, once perplex'd with Thorn,
The spiry Firr and shapely Box adorn;
To leafless Shrubs the flow'ring Palms succeed,
And od'rous Myrtle to the noisome Weed.
The Lambs with Wolves shall graze the verdant Mead,
And Boys in flow'ry Bands the Tyger lead;
The Steer and Lion at one Crib shall meet,
And harmless Serpents lick the Pilgrim's Feet.
The smiling Infant in his Hand shall take
The crested Basilisk and speckled Snake;
Pleas'd the green Lustre of the Scales survey,
And with their forky Tongue shall innocently play.
Rise, crown'd with Light, imperial *Salem* rise!
Exalt thy tow'ry Head, and lift thy Eyes!
See, a long Race thy spacious Courts adorn;
See future Sons and Daughters yet unborn
In crowding Ranks on ev'ry Side arise,
Demanding Life, impatient for the Skies!
See barb'rous Nations at thy Gates attend,
Walk in thy Light, and in thy Temple bend;
See thy bright Altars throng'd with prostrate Kings,
And heap'd with Products of *Sabaean* Springs!
For thee *Idume's* spicy Forests blow,
And seeds of Gold in *Ophyr's* Mountains glow.
See Heav'n its sparkling Portals wide display,
And break upon thee in a Flood of Day!
No more the rising *Sun* shall gild the Morn,
Nor Evening *Cynthia* fill her silver Horn,
But lost, dissolv'd in thy superior Rays,
One Tyde of Glory, one unclouded Blaze,
O'erflow thy Courts: The LIGHT HIMSELF shall shine
Reveal'd, and *God's* eternal Day be thine!
The Seas shall waste, the Skies in Smoke decay,
Rocks fall to Dust, and Mountains melt away;
But fix'd *His* Word, *His* saving Pow'r remains:
Thy *Realm* for ever lasts! Thy own *Messiah* reigns!

Messia

Tollite concentum, *Solymaeae* tollite nymphae!
Nil mortale loquor, coelum mihi carminis alta

Materies; poscunt gravius coelestia plectrum.
Muscosi fontes, silvestria tecta, valete,
Aonidesque Deae, et mendacis somnia *Pindi.*
Tu mihi, qui flamma movisti pectora sancti
Siderea *Isaiae,* dignos accende furores!
  Immatura calens rapitur per saecula vates,
Sic orsus—Qualis rerum mihi nascitur ordo!
Virgo! virgo parit! felix radicibus arbor
Jessaeis surgit, mulcentesque aethera flores
Coelestes lambunt animae; ramisque columba,
Nuncia sacra Dei, plaudentibus insidet alis.
Nectareos rores, alimentaque mitia coelum
Praebeat, et tacite foecundos irriget imbres!
Huc foedat quos lepra, urit quos febris, adeste!
Dia salutares spirant medicamina rami.
Hic requies fessis; non sacra saevit in umbra
Vis boreae gelida, aut rapidi violentia solis.
"Irrita vanescent priscae vestigia fraudis,"
Justitiaeque manus pretio intemerata bilancem
Attollet reducis; bellis praetendet olivas
Compositis Pax alma suas, terrasque revisens
Sedatas niveo Virtus lucebit amictu.
Volvantur celeres anni! Lux purpuret ortum
Expectata diu! Naturae claustra refringens
Nascere, magne puer! Tibi primas, ecce! corollas
Deproperat tellus, fundit tibi munera, quicquid
Carpit *Arabs,* hortis quicquid frondescit eois.
Altius, en! *Lebanon* gaudentia culmina tollit,
En! summo exultant nutantes vertice silvae.
Mittit aromaticas vallis *Saronica* nubes,
Et juga *Carmeli* recreant fragrantia coelum.
Deserti laeta mollescunt aspera voce,
Auditur Deus! ecce Deus! reboantia circum
Saxa sonant Deus; ecce deus! deflectitur aether
Demissumque Deum tellus capit; ardua cedrus
Gloria silvarum, dominum inclinata salutet!
Surgite convalles, tumidi subsidite montes!
Sternite saxa viam, rapidi discedite fluctus!
En! quem turba diu cecinerunt enthea, vates,
En! SALVATOR adest; vultus agnoscite caeci
Divinos, surdas sacra vox permulceat aures!
Ille cutim spissam visus hebetare vetabit,

Reclusisque oculis infundet amabile lumen,
Obstrictasque diu linguas in carmina solvet.
Ille vias vocis pandet, flexusque liquentis
Harmoniae purgata novos mirabitur auris.
Accrescunt tremulis tactu nova robora nervis:
Consuetus fulcro innixus reptare bacilli
Jam saltu capreas, jam cursu provocat euros.
Non planctus, non moesta sonant suspiria, pectus
Singultans mulcet, lachrymantes terget ocellos.
Vincla coercebunt luctantem adamantina mortem,
Aeternoque orci dominator vulnere languens
Invalidi raptos sceptri plorabit honores.
Ut qua dulce strepunt scatebrae, qua laeta virescunt
Pascua, qua blandum spirat purissimus aer
Pastor agit pecudes, teneros modo suscipit agnos,
Et gremio fotis selectas porrigit herbas,
Amissas modo quaerit oves, revocatque vagantes;
Fidus adest custos, seu nox furat horrida nimbis,
Sive dies medius morientia torreat arva:
Postera sic pastor divinus secla beabit,
Et curas felix patrias testabitur orbis.
Non ultra infestis concurrent agmina signis,
Hostiles oculis flammas jaculantia torvis;
Non litui accendent bellum, non campus ahenis
Triste coruscabit radiis; dabit hasta recusa
Vomerem, et in falcem rigidus curvabitur ensis.
Atria, pacis opus, surgent, finemque caduci
Natus ad optatum perducet coepta parentis.
Qui duxit sulcos, illi teret area messem,
Et serae texent vites umbracula proli.
Attoniti dumeta vident inculta coloni
Suave rubere rosis, sitientesque inter arenas
Garrula mirantur salientis murmura rivi.
Per saxa, ignivomi nuper spelaea draconis,
Canna viret, juncique tremit mutabilis umbra.
Horruit implexo qua vallis sente, figurae
Surgit amans abies teretis, buxique sequaces
Artificis frondent dextrae; palmisque rubeta
Aspera, odoratae cedunt mala gramina myrto.
Per valles sociata lupo lasciviet agna,
Cumque leone petet tutus praesepe juvencus.

Florea mansuetae petulantes vincula tigri
Per ludum pueri injicient, et fessa colubri
Membra viatoris recreabunt frigore linguae.
Serpentes teneris nil jam lethale minantes
Tractabit palmis infans, motusque trisulcae
Ridebit linguae innocuos, squamasque virentes
Aureaque admirans rutilantis fulgura cristae.
Indue reginam, turritae frontis honores
Tolle, *Salema,* sacros, quam circum gloria pennas
Explicat, incinctam radiatae luce tiarae!
En! formosa tibi porrecta per atria proles
Ordinibus surgit densis, vitamque requirit
Impatiens, lenteque fluentes increpat annos.
Ecce! peregrinis fervent tua limina turbis;
Barbarus, en! clarum divino lumine templum
Ingreditur, cultuque tuo mansuescere gaudet.
Cinnameos cumulos, *Nabathaei* munera veris,
Ecce! cremant genibus tritae regalibus arae.
Solis *Ophyraeis* crudum tibi montibus aurum
Maturant radii, tibi balsama sudat *Idume.*
Aetheris, en! portas sacro fulgore micantes
Caelicolae pandunt, torrentisque aurea lucis
Flumina prorumpunt; non posthac sole rubescet
India nascenti, placidaeve argentea noctis
Luna vices revehet; radios pater ipse diei
Proferet archetypos; coelestis gaudia lucis
Ipso fonte bibes, quae circumfusa beatam
Regiam inundabit, nullis cessura tenebris.
Littora deficiens arentia deseret aequor,
Sidera fumabunt, diro labefacta tremore
Saxa cadent, solidique liquescent robora montis:
Tu secura tamen confusa elementa videbis,
Laetaque *Messia* semper dominabere rege,
Pollicitis firmata Dei, stabilita ruinis.

Raise the chorus, nymphs of Solyma, raise it! I speak no mortal theme. Heaven is the lofty matter of my song; heavenly things call for a more serious plectrum. Mossy springs, woodland dwellings, farewell, and ye Aonian goddesses, and the dreams of fanciful Pindus **(5).** You, I beg you, you who stirred the heart of holy Isaiah with sidereal flame, kindle a worthy madness!

The bard on fire, carried through ages that are yet to come to pass, began thus: What a train of events do I see coming to birth! A virgin! A virgin is giving birth! From Jesse's root a blessed tree is rising, and the celestial spirit plays around its blooms, caressing the air. On its branches the dove, sacred messenger of God, settles with clapping wings. May heaven bring forth dewy nectar and gentle sustenance, and silently rain down fertile showers. Come here all who are disfigured by leprosy or burnt by fever! The health-giving branches exude divine medicines. Here is rest for the weary; in its sacred shade the chilling force of the north wind does not rage or the violence of the scorching sun. "The traces of our ancient sin will fade away into nothingness", and the hand of Justice, who will then have returned, will hold aloft the balance unsullied by bribery. Wars shall be brought to an end, benign Peace will hold forth her olive-branch, and Righteousness shining in her snowy robe will come back to the quiet earth. May the years roll swiftly by! May the long-expected day redden the morning sky! Come to birth, o mighty boy, bursting the bars of Nature! See! For you the earth hastens to bring her first garlands, and pours forth gifts—whatever the Arab picks, whatever blooms in the orchards of the east. Look! Lebanon is raising higher his joyful peaks. Look! The forests are waving in joy on the mountain tops. Sharon's valley sends forth scented clouds, and the summit of Carmel refreshes the sky with its fragrance. The roughness of the desert grows smooth hearing that joyful voice. God is heard approaching! See, God is here! On every side the cliffs shout aloud reechoing "God; behold, God is here!" Heaven stoops down and the earth receives God as he descends; the tall cedar, the glory of the woods, bows its head to greet the Lord! Rise up, you valleys, sink down, you proud hills! You rocks, smooth his path. Make way you rushing waves! Look! He of whom the inspired company of bards has been singing, look! The SAVIOUR is here. You who are blind, behold his heavenly face; let his holy voice charm the ears of the deaf! He will forbid a film of darkness to blunt your vision, and will open your eyes, pouring in his kindly light; he will loosen tongues that have long been bound, producing song. He will open up a pathway for the voice, and the ear, now cleansed, will be astonished at the unfamiliar rise and fall of flowing harmony. New strength is given to the touch of shaking fingers; he who is used to creeping along, leaning on a stick for support, now leaps like a deer, now runs like the wind. No lamentation, no sad sighs are heard; he soothes the sobbing breast, and wipes the tears from every eye. Bonds of adamant will confine struggling death, and the lord of hell, weakened by an everlasting wound, will lament the lost glory of his now powerless scepter.

Like the shepherd who drives his flocks where sweet waters babble, where the glad pastures are green, where the purest air breathes pleasantly, now taking up the young lambs and offering them the choicest grasses as they nestle in his arms, now going in search of lost sheep and calling back those which have strayed, a faithful ever-present guardian, whether by night a rough rainstorm rages or the noonday heat scorches the dying fields, so the holy shepherd will bring blessings to future ages, and the happy world will bear witness to his fatherly care. No more will battle lines clash with their hostile standards, hurling flames of hatred from their fierce eyes; trumpets will not light the fires of war, the plain will not flash balefully with rays of bronze; the spearhead reforged will serve as a ploughshare, and the tough sword will be bent to form a sickle. Palaces, those structures of peace, will rise, and the son will bring to the desired end what was begun by his short-lived father. The floor will thresh the harvest for him who ploughed the furrows, and in years to come the vines will weave a shade for his offspring. Farmers watch in amazement as rough thickets grow red with sweet-smelling roses, and they marvel as streams spring up with chattering gurgles amid thirsty sands. Among rocks that were recently the lair of the fire-breathing dragon rushes grow green, and the ever-changing shadow of the reed waves to and fro. In the rough valley tangled with thorns the fir springs up fondly rejoicing in its elegant shape, and box trees that obey the carver's hand burst into leaf; rough scrub gives way to palms, and poisonous herbs to fragrant myrtle. Throughout the valleys the lamb will play in the company of the wolf, and along with the lion the steer will make safely for his stall. Cheeky boys, for a joke, will throw ropes of flowers on the gentle tiger, and snakes will refresh the traveler's weary limbs with their cool tongues. The infant will take in his soft hands serpents that no longer carry the threat of death, and he will smile at the harmless flickerings of their three-forked tongues, and gaze in wonder at their green scales and the golden flashes of their glowing crests. Put on the queen's regalia, Salem, raise the sacred dignity of your towered brow, round which glory spreads her wings, encircled as it is by the light of the flashing tiara! Look! Throughout your spacious halls beautiful future offspring are coming up in dense rows, impatiently demanding life and reproaching the years for gliding by so slowly. See! Your thresholds swarm with crowds of foreign people; look! the barbarian is entering the temple that shines with a holy light, happy to become cultivated through your worship. See! The altars that are worn down by the knees of kings are burning heaps of cinnamon, the gift of the Nabathean spring. For you the sun's rays are maturing crude gold in the mountains of

Ophir. Idume exudes balsam in your honour. Look! The heavenly host is throwing open the doors of the sky, which glint with holy splendour, and golden rivers of rushing light burst forth. After this India will not grow red with the rising sun, nor will the silver moon bring round the succession of quiet nights. The father himself will bring forth his own beams of day; you will drink from the original fountain the joys of celestial light, which spreading all round will flood upon the holy palace and never give way to darkness. The sea will dwindle and withdraw from the shores, leaving them dry; the stars will go up in smoke; the cliffs will tumble down shaken by the awful convulsion, and the hardness of the solid mountain will dissolve. You, however, will witness in safety the confusion of the elements, and with the Messiah as king you will remain happily in power for ever, firmly based on the promise of God, unmoved within a falling world.

The poem is written in hexameters throughout. In the following notes V stands for Virgil. I have disregarded some phrases borrowed from other sources. Johnson's modifications of Pope are discussed by O'Sullivan (1975, 579–91).

1. *Solyma* is Jerusalem. **2.** Horace had said "nil mortale loquar" when inspired by Bacchus to celebrate Augustus (*Odes* 3.25.18). **4–5.** The poets abandon the setting of classical pastoral and the figures of the Aonian goddesses, i.e., the Muses, who frequented Mt. Helicon in Aonia (Boeotia), in favor of a Christian theme. Pindus was a mountain on the borders of Thessaly and Macedonia associated with the Muses. *Mendacis* ("lying") is probably used in the weaker sense of "fanciful." The "dreams" may refer to the tradition in which poets fall asleep and receive divine inspiration; the original example was Hesiod, who was inspired by the Muses beneath Mount Helicon (*Theogony,* 22–34). **9.** Johnson is thinking of V.*Ecl.*4.5 "Magnus ab integro saeclorum nascitur ordo." Johnson's new order is that which followed the birth of Christ. **10.** Cf. Isaiah.7.14. Johnson has been faulted for writing Virgō followed by Virgŏ. **10–11.** For Jesse's root see Isaiah.11.1. **12.** The dove, a symbol of the Holy Ghost, is present by implication in Isaiah.11.2, and explicitly in Matt. 3:16 and John 1.32. Hence Pope's "Mystic Dove." **13.** In 'the sacred messenger of God' Johnson is thinking of the dove's presence in pictures of the annunciation. **16–19.** Cf. Isaiah.25.4. **20.** The line combines elements of V.*Ecl.*4.14 and 4.31. **26.** Lucretius speaks of Epicurus as eager to be the first to burst through the tight bars of nature's gates: "effringere ut arta / naturae primus portarum claustra cupiret" (*De Rerum Natura* 1.70–71). The reminiscence is poetically, if not religiously, appropriate. **27–29.** Cf. V.*Ecl.*4.18–25. **30.** Lebanon: a mountainous region on the coast of Syria. **32–34.** Mt. Carmel on the coast of Palestine south of Haifa; Sharon a coastal plain south of Mt. Carmel; Isaiah.35.1–2. **35.** Cf. V.*Ecl.*5.64. **37–40.** Cf. Isaiah.40.3–4.

42–51. Cf. Isaiah.35.5–6. **53–54.** Cf. Isaiah.25.8. **59–60.** Cf. Isaiah.40.11. **69–70.** Cf. V. *Georgics* 1.508, Isaiah.2.4. *recudo* is not found in classical Latin. **75–79.** Cf. V.*Ecl*.4.28–30, Isaiah.35.7. **80–83.** Cf. Isaiah.41.19. "Spiry" had no Latin equivalent; Johnson transferred Pope's "shapely" from Box to Fir (*teretis*). **84–92.** Cf. V.*Ecl*.4.19–25, Isaiah.11.6–8. **96–98.** The poets seem to be thinking of the scene in *Aeneid* 6.719–21, where the souls in Hades are eager to return to the world above. **102.** The Nabathaeans lived in north Arabia. **104.** Ophir: a region famous for its gold; its location is uncertain, but is thought to have been in either south or east Arabia. **105.** Idume: the biblical Edom in south Palestine. **107–8.** Johnson has reversed the natural phrase "rushing rivers of golden light." **108–11.** Cf. Isaiah.60.19–20. **114–19.** Cf. Isaiah.51.6, 54.10.

O.55–56, Y.40–41, B.37

Ad Urbanum

Urbane, nullis fesse laboribus,
Urbane, nullis victe calumniis,
Cui fronte sertum in erudita
Perpetuo viret et virebit;

Quid moliatur gens imitantium,
Quid et minetur, sollicitus parum,
Vacare solis perge Musis,
Juxta animo studiisque felix.

Linguae procacis plumbea spicula,
Fidens, superbo frange silentio;
Victrix per obstantes catervas
sedulitas animosa tendet.

Intende nervos fortis, inanibus
Risurus olim nisibus aemuli;
Intende iam nervos, habebis
Participes operae Camoenas.

Non ulla Musis pagina gratior
Quam quae severis ludicra iungere
Novit, fatigatamque nugis
Utilibus recreare mentem.

Texente Nymphis serta Lycoride,
Rosae ruborem sic viola adjuvat
  Immista, sic Iris refulget
    Aethereis variata fucis.

To Urbanus

Urbanus, unwearied by any toil, Urbanus unconquered by any calumnies, on whose learned brow the garland is and will remain for ever green, you who are wholly indifferent to whatever the tribe of imitators may devise and whatever threats they may utter, continue to make time for the Muses alone, happy alike in your mind and occupation. Be confident enough to break the leaden arrows of impudent tongues by a dignified silence; your courage and diligence will walk victoriously through the crowds that seek to bar your way. Boldly flex your muscles; some day you will laugh at the vain endeavours of your rival. Now flex your muscles, you will have the Camenae as collaborators in your work. No page is more welcome to the Muses than that which knows how to combine grave and gay, and to refresh the weary mind with helpful trifles. In that way, when Lycoris is weaving garlands for the Nymphs, a mixture of violets sets off the rose's red; in that way Iris shines forth in the various colours of the rainbow.

This meter is named Alcaic after Alcaeus (late seventh–sixth century BC) from Mytilene on Lesbos. He was the poet with whom Horace felt the closest affinity.

The scheme is as follows:

⏓ — ⏑ — — — ⏑⏑ — ⏑ ⏓
⏓ — ⏑ — — — ⏑⏑ — ⏑ ⏓
⏓ — ⏑ — — — ⏑ — ⏓
— ⏑⏑ — ⏑⏑ — ⏑ — ⏓

1. "Urbanus" (sophisticated gentleman), is applied to Edward Cave, publisher of the *Gentleman's Magazine.* **9.** In Ovid, *Met.* 1.468ff. Cupid is said to have had two arrows, one of gold, which he fired at Apollo, and the other of lead, which struck

Daphne, making her insensible to Apollo's advances. Here the critics' leaden arrows have no effect on Cave. **11.** Johnson has in mind Horace, *Odes* 4.9.43–4: "per obstantis catervas / explicuit sua victor arma," where the honest man "carries his weapons victoriously through the hosts that are ranged against him." In *tendet* (12) there is also a hint of Regulus, who has made a path through the crowd, and is going to meet his death in Carthage as calmly as if he were "making his way" (*tendens*) to Venafrum or Tarentum (*Odes* 3.5.50–56). **18.** The mixture of grave and gay was especially characteristic of Horace. It is made explicit in connection with satyr plays in *Ars Poetica* 226 "vertere seria ludo."

O.57, Y.44, B.44

Ad Ricardum Savage, Arm.
Humani Generis Amatorem

Humani studium generis cui pectore fervet,
O! colat humanum te foveatque genus!

To Richard Savage Esq.
Lover of the Human Race

You, whose heart burns with devotion for the human race, O may the human race revere and cherish you!

Title: *Arm.* is short for *armiger,* "Bearer of a coat-of-arms," hence "esquire."

O.57, Y.45, B.45

In Elizae Aenigma

Quis formae modus imperio? Venus arrogat audax
Omnia, nec curae sunt sua sceptra Jovi.
Ab Jove Maeonides descendere somnia narrat:
Haec veniunt Cypriae somnia missa Deae.
Jupiter unus erat, qui stravit fulmine gentes;
Nunc armant Veneris lumina tela Jovis.

On Elizabeth's Riddle

What end will there be to the power of beauty? Venus in her insolence lays claim to everything; and his bolts are no longer in Jove's charge. Maeonides relates that dreams come down from Jove; these dreams come despatched by the Cyprian Goddess. Jupiter was the only one who laid low whole peoples with his thunderbolt; now Venus's bright eyes arm the weapons of Jove.

Title: The piece is a reply to a long riddle in English by Johnson's friend Elizabeth Carter in the *Gentleman's Magazine* of Feb. 1738. Johnson also wrote a version in Greek, but the two pieces are too similar to justify printing the text and translation of both. **3.** Maeonides: the Lydian. Several centers in Maeonia or Lydia (a country in the west of Asia Minor) claimed to be the birthplace of Homer. **4.** The Cyprian Goddess is Venus.

O.58, Y.63, B.51

To Elizabeth Carter

Quid mihi cum cultu? Probitas inculta nitescit,
   Et juvat ingenii vita sine arte rudis.
Ingenium et mores si pulchra probavit Elisa,
   Quid majus mihi spes ambitiosa dabit?

What have I to do with adornment? Integrity shines forth unadorned, and the simple life of the mind gives pleasure without contrivance. If the lovely Elizabeth approves of my mind and character, what greater prize will my lofty aspirations offer me?

This piece, in Johnson's writing but without a title, was found among Mrs. Carter's papers. **1.** Propertius (1.2) urges his beloved to ignore foreign adornments (Coan silk, Syrian perfume, etc.); her natural beauty cannot be enhanced. Some other treatments of the same topic are noted by Enk (1946, 2:19–21), including Plautus, *Mostellaria* 288–92 and Paulus Silentiarius, *Palatine Anthology* 5.270. Johnson gives the theme an ethical slant.

O.59, Y.43, B.41

To a Lady who Spoke in Defence of Liberty

Liber ut esse velim, suasisti, pulchra Maria:
Ut maneam liber, pulchra Maria, vale.

Lovely Mary, you have convinced me that I should wish to be free: that I may *remain* free, lovely Mary, goodbye.

This piece, with the English title, appeared in the *Gentleman's Magazine* of April 1738. The *London Magazine* of the following year has the improved word order *liber maneam.* A Latin heading was added in 1787. Mary ("Molly") Aston was a lady of Whiggish opinions.

2
Poems, 1738–1749

O.82, Y.61, B.49

Ad Elisam Popi Horto Lauros Carpentem

Elysios Popi dum ludit laeta per hortos,
  En avida lauros carpit Elisa manu.
Nil opus est furto. Lauros tibi, dulcis Elisa,
  Si neget optatas Popus, Apollo dabit.

To Eliza Plucking Laurel in Pope's Garden

While she plays happily in Pope's heavenly garden, see, Eliza plucks laurel leaves with a greedy hand. No theft is needed. If Pope should refuse the laurels you desire, sweet Eliza, Apollo will give them.

For information about Pope's garden at Twickenham see Mack (1985, 362 and note on 879).

O.84, Y.63, B.52

Εἰς ΒΙΡΧΙΟΝ

Εἶδεν Ἀληθείη πρῴην χαίρουσα γράφοντα
  Ἡρώων τε βίους Βίρχιον, ἠδὲ Σοφῶν,
Καὶ βίον, εἶπεν, ὅταν ῥίψῃς θανάτοιο βέλεσσι,
  Σοῦ ποτε γραψόμενον Βίρχιον ἄλλον ἔχοις.

Recently Truth rejoiced on seeing Birch writing the lives of heroes and sages. "When," she said, "you cast down your life before the darts of death, may you have another Birch to write yours."

Ξοῦ is somewhat awkward, but unless it is interpreted in this way the epigram lacks point.

(O.448, Y.63, B.52

In Birchium

Arte nova, raraque fide perscripserat ausus
  Birchius egregios, claraque gesta virum.
Hunc oculis Veri Fautrix lustravit acutis,
  Et placido tandem haec edidit ore, Dea:
"Pergo modo, atque tuas olim post funera laudes
  Qui scribat meritas, Birchius alter erit."

On Thomas Birch

In a new style, and with rare accuracy, Birch had the enterprise to write about distinguished men and their glorious deeds. The Patroness of Truth looked at him with her sharp eyes, and eventually the Goddess spoke thus with her calm voice: "Just carry on, and after your death there will be another Birch to write your well-deserved praises.")

The Latin epigram is included by O among *Poems of Doubtful Authorship.* (In v. 2 *egregius* is obviously a misprint.) The case for attributing it to Johnson is very weak. B (52–53) sets out the pros and cons. There are two considerations that neither edition mentions. First, the Latin version misses the point (and therefore the raison d'être) of the epigram, viz. the double meaning of "life"; secondly, the style is prolix (the clumsy relation of *egregios* to *virum,* the padding in the fourth line, and the extra couplet). For Johnson's sake it should be regarded as spurious.

O.85–86, Y.64–65, B.63–64

Post-Genitis

Cum lapidem hunc, magni
Qui nunc jacet incola stagni,

Vel pede equus tanget,
Vel arator vomere franget,

Sentiet aegra metus,
Effundet patria fletus,

Littoraque ut fluctu,
Resonabunt oppida luctu:

Nam foecunda rubri
Serpent per prata colubri,

Gramina vastantes,
Flores fructusque vorantes,

Omnia foedantes,
Vitiantes, et spoliantes;

Quanquam haud pugnaces,
Ibunt per cuncta minaces,

Fures absque timore,
Et pingues absque labore,

Horrida dementes
Rapiet discordia gentes,

Plurima tunc leges
Mutabit, plurima reges

Natio, conversa
In rabiem tunc contremet Ursa

Cynthia, tunc latis
Florebunt lilia pratis,

Nec fremere audebit
Leo, sed violare timebit,

Omnia consuetus
Populari pascua laetus.

Ante oculos natos
Calcatos et cruciatos

Jam feret ignavus,
Vetitaque libidine pravus.

En quoque quod mirum,
Quod dicas denique dirum,

Sanguinem equus sugit,
Neque bellua victa remugit.

To Posterity

(Johnson's translation)

Whene'er this Stone, now hid beneath the Lake,
The Horse shall trample, or the Plough shall break,
Then, O my Country! shalt thou groan distrest,
Grief swell thine Eyes, and Terror chill thy Breast.
Thy Streets with Violence of Woe shall sound,
Loud as the Billows bursting on the Ground.
Then thro' thy Fields shall scarlet Reptiles stray,
And Rapine and Pollution mark their Way.
Their hungry Swarms the peaceful Vale shall fright
Still fierce to threaten, still afraid to fight;
The teeming Year's whole Product shall devour,
Insatiate pluck the fruit, and crop the flow'r:
Shall glutton on the industrious Peasants Spoil,
Rob without Fear, and fatten without Toil.
Then o'er the World shall Discord stretch her Wings,
Kings change their Laws, and Kingdoms change their Kings.
The Bear enrag'd th' affrighted Moon shall dread;
The Lilies o'er the Vales triumphant spread;
Nor shall the Lyon, wont of old to reign
Despotic o'er the desolated Plain,
Henceforth th' inviolable Bloom invade,
Or dare to murmur in the flow'ry Glade;
His tortur'd Sons shall die before his Face,

While he lies melting in a lewd Embrace;
And, yet more strange! his Veins a Horse shall drain,
Nor shall the passive Coward once complain.

Dating from 1739, these verses are presented as "an ancient prophetical inscription, in monkish rhyme, lately discovered near Lynn in Norfolk." Along with an ironical commentary, they make up the so-called *Marmor Norfolciense,* an attack on Walpole, who was MP for Lynn Regis (King's Lynn) and the Brunswick succession. The commentator, who styles himself Probus Britannicus ("Upright Briton"), takes the name of Marcus Valerius Probus, a famous scholar of the late first century AD. Reading the subversive text, he shows disapproval, sometimes amounting to shock. As Greene (1977, 20) says, "His persona is that of a seemingly well-intentioned but not very bright defender of what the author wishes to attack." Pope is said to have enjoyed the piece, but modern readers tend to agree with those who found the irony rather heavy-handed.

The "monkish rhymes" consist of rhyming couplets, each made up of the first and second parts of a hexameter. Speaking of the ninth-century poet Gottschalk, Raby says that "he naturally took a classical metre, and by adding rime made something new and strange" (1.1957, 226); a passage of his leonine rhymes addressed to Ratramnus is quoted on 228, beginning "nimium metuo tibi respondere quod imo / in sensu teneo, quia torpeo pectora bruto," and another passage in the same form written by an anonymous contemporary is quoted on 229.

7. The "scarlet reptiles" represent the red coats of the standing army, so disliked by Johnson. Some readers hear an echo of Virgil, *Aeneid* 2.205ff., which describe how two snakes with red crests and blood-red eyes kill Laocoon and his sons. **13.** "Peasants," without the apostrophe, represented the possessive plural. **15–16.** A reference not only to the deposition of James II but to the wars of succession to the Spanish, Polish, and Austrian thrones, and the change of dynasties in Lorraine, Tuscany, Parma, and the two Sicilies. **16.** The Latin means "Many a nation will change its laws, many a nation its kings" (21–23). **17.** In the Latin *conversa . . . Ursa* (23–24) is ablative, *contremet* (24) is intransitive. The Empress of Russia's dominions lay under the constellation of the Bear. The moon refers to the Turkish empire. **18.** The lilies represent the advance of French power. **19–20.** The British lion's former conquests in France. **22.** In the Latin the lion does not dare *fremere.* Johnson has taken this in the sense of "growl"; for "to murmur" he has in his dictionary "to give a low shrill sound," and he quotes Pope "The forests murmur and the surges roar." This is in line with the fact that the verb could cover something less subdued than our "murmur." The Latin *murmur* could sometimes even mean "a roar," as in Martial 8.53.1, where it describes the sound of lions in a forest. These considerations mean that there is no bathos intended in Johnson's translation. **23.** A reference to the cutting off of Jenkins's ear by the Spaniards in 1731. **24.** The "lewd embrace" alludes to George II's liaison with Amalie von Wallmoden. **25.** The "horse" is the white horse, i.e., the badge of the Guelph house, from which the Hanoverians were descended. The commentator finds such an imputation detestable.

O.93, Y.76, B.58

Verses on a grotto by the river Thames at Twickenham composed of marbles, spars, and minerals. By Mr Pope. Latine redditum.

The original runs as follows:

Thou who shalt stop, where *Thames*' translucent wave
Shines a broad mirrour thro' the shadowy cave;
Where lingering drops from mineral roofs distill,
And pointed crystals break the sparkling rill,
Unpolish'd gemms no ray on pride bestow,
And latent metals innocently glow:
Approach. Great Nature studiously behold!
And eye the mine without a wish for gold.
Approach: but aweful! Lo th' *Aegerian* grott,
where, nobly-pensive, St. John sate and thought;
Where *British* sighs from dying Wyndham stole,
And the bright flame was shot thro' Marchmont's soul.
Let such, such only, tread this sacred floor,
Who dare to love their country, and be poor.

Quisquis iter tendis, vitreas qua lucidus undas
Speluncae late *Thamesis* praetendit opacae,
Marmoreo trepidant qua lentae in fornice guttae,
Crystallisque latex fractus scintillat acutis,
Gemmaque luxuriae nondum famulata nitenti
Splendet, et incoquitur tectum sine fraude metallum:
Ingredere O!—Magnam pura cole mente parentem,
Auriferasque, auri metuens, scrutare cavernas.
Ingredere! *Egeriae* sacrum en tibi panditur antrum!
Hic, in se totum longe per opaca futuri
Temporis *Henricum* rapuit vis vivida mentis;

Hic pia *Vindamius* traxit suspiria, in ipsa
Morte memor patriae; hic *Marcmonti* pectore prima
Coelestis fido caluerunt semina flammae.
Temnere opes pretium sceleris, patriamque tueri
Fortis, ades, solus tangas venerabile limen.

See the descriptions and illustrations in Mack (1985, 362–65). **6.** *splendet* (in the transcript made by or for Thomas Percy c.1775 and presumably sanctioned by Johnson) is an improvement on *pendet.* Pope v. 6 is an allusion to Horace, *Odes* 3.3.49–50: "aurum inrepertum et sic melius situm, / cum terra celat" [gold which is undiscovered and better so placed when the earth conceals it]. The idea of "glow" may owe something to *Odes* 2.2.3–4, where silver is said to be despised by the addressee unless it shines in moderate use; "temperato / *splendeat* usu." **9.** The grotto of the nymph Egeria, who is said to have advised King Numa, was near the Porta Capena (Livy 1.19, Juvenal 3.12). **11.** Henry St. John, Viscount Bolingbroke (1678–1751) A distinguished Tory who led the opposition to Walpole and attacked him in *The Craftsman.* After 1723 he was a neighbor of Pope, who much admired him for his intellect and eloquence. Speaking of the grotto, Pope says "There, my retreat the best companions grace, / Chiefs, out of war, and statesmen, out of place. / There St. John mingles with my friendly bowl, / The feast of reason and the flow of soul." Johnson alludes to his intellect in a phrase taken from Lucretius's praise of Epicurus: "vis vivida mentis" (*De Rerum Natura* 1.72). For a general study see I. Kramnik, *Bolingbroke and his Circle,* 1968. It is relevant to add that Pope's *Essay on Man,* which he dedicated to Bolingbroke, was intended to be read "at least in some degree, as a modern *De Rerum Natura*" (Mack 1985, 525; for bibliographical support see his note on 898). **12.** Sir William Wyndham (1687–1740), another opponent of Walpole's; a respected, if not a brilliant, figure. For his "British sighs" cf. Pope's line "And thy last sigh [i.e., Britain's] was heard when Wyndham died" (*1740,* 80). Johnson's poem appeared the following year. **13.** Hugh Hume, third Earl of Marchmont (1708–94), another member of the opposition. Pope admired his integrity, and subsequently appointed him one of his executors; in *1740,* 74–75 he (as Lord Polworth) and his father are mentioned among those who were trying to save Britain. All these figures styled themselves as Patriots, defending English liberty; so the "bright flame" is that of patriotism.

3
Poems, 1750–1784

O.180, Y.266–67, B.71–2

In Theatro

Tertii verso quater orbe lustri,
Quid theatrales tibi, Crispe, pompae?
Quam decet canos male literatos
  Sera voluptas!

Tene mulceri fidibus canoris?
Tene cantorum modulis stupere?
Tene per pictas oculo elegante
  Currere formas?

Inter equales, sine felle liber,
Codices, veri studiosus, inter
Rectius vives, sua quisque carpat
  Gaudia gratus.

Lusibus gaudet puer otiosis,
Luxus oblectat juvenem theatri,
At seni fluxo sapienter uti
  Tempore restat.

In the Theater

Now that the circle of your third half-decade has turned four times, what are theatrical extravaganzas to you, Crisp? How unseemly for well-read grey hairs is such a pleasure so late in life! You, beguiled by tuneful strings! You, entranced by the ditties of singers! You, running a discriminating eye over painted figures! Much better for you to live among men of your own age, detached and without rancor, searching for the truth in ancient volumes. Everyone should gratefully seize the pleasures that are proper for him. A boy enjoys carefree games, a young man is charmed by the lavishness of the theater; but it remains for an old man to use his time wisely as it passes.

The poem is in Sapphics, the scheme being as follows:

— ∪ — — — ∪∪ — ∪ — ⏓
— ∪ — — — ∪∪ — ∪ — ⏓
— ∪ — — — ∪∪ — ∪ — ⏓
— ∪∪ — ⏓

This is a common meter in Horace (and therefore appropriate to this very Horatian piece), but rare in Johnson. The date is 1771.

The tone of the first two stanzas resembles that of *Odes* 1.29, in which Horace teases Iccius for taking part in a military expedition for the sake of plunder. **1.** A *lustrum* was a period of five years. Horace uses it ruefully to record his age in *Odes* 2.4.24 and 4.1.6. **2.** Horace addresses a Crispus in *Odes* 2.2.3, which is also in Sapphics. B suggests that Johnson's Crispus may refer to the dramatist Samuel Crisp (1708–83). This interesting idea is borne out by one of Crisp's letters that speaks of a visit from the Thrales and Dr. Johnson. The link was Fanny Burney; see Hutton (1905, 46). **7–8.** What are the painted figures? Perhaps the actors with their costumes and makeup; or possibly the stage set. **11–12.** "Rectius vives" is the beginning of a famous ode on observing the golden mean (2.10). **15.** The idea that certain lifestyles are appropriate to certain ages is explored in a famous passage of Horace's *Ars Poetica* 156–78. "Sapienter uti" occurs in *Odes* 4.9.48.

O.182–3, Y. 287–8, B.93

Psalm 117

1. O praise the Lord, all ye nations: praise him, all ye people.
2. For his merciful kindness is great toward us: and the truth of the Lord endureth for ever. Praise ye the Lord. (Authorized Version)

Psalmus 117

Anni qua volucris ducitur orbita
Patrem coelicolum perpetuo *colant*
  Quovis sanguine cretae
    Gentes undique carmine.
Patrem cujus amor blandior in dies
Mortales miseros servat, alit, fovet,
  Omnes undique Gentes
    Sancto dicite carmine.

Wherever the circle of the swift year revolves, let the nations, from whatever blood they be born, praise the Father of the heavenly host everywhere in perpetual song.

All ye peoples everywhere, hymn in sacred song the Father whose love, more tender every day, saves, feeds, and cherishes wretched mortals.

The stanzas consist of two lesser Asclepiads (— — — ∪∪ — — ∪∪ — ∪ ⏓) followed by a Pherecratic (— — — ∪∪ — ⏓) followed in turn by a Glyconic (— — — ∪∪ — ∪ ⏓).

According to a note by Johnson, the piece was written in bed. The first verse of the psalm is in essence an exhortation; this effect is spoilt if we read the traditional *colunt* (2); I have therefore emended it to *colant* (an imperfectly closed *a* could easily have been transcribed as a *u*). This brings the tone into line with the imperative *dicite* in v. 8.

6. "Wretched mortals" is a set phrase in Homer (δειλοῖσι βροτοῖσι).

O.184, Y.270, B.70

Versus Collari Caprae Domini Banks Inscribendi

Perpetui, ambita bis terra, praemia lactis
  Haec habet altrici Capra secunda Jovis.

Lines to be Inscribed on the Collar of the Goat that Belongs to Banks

Having sailed twice around the world, this goat, which is second only to Jove's nurse, has her reward for her unfailing supply of milk.

The goat is said to have accompanied Capt. Wallis in the Dolphin (1766–68) and Capt. Cook in the Endeavour (1768–71). Sir Joseph Banks was present on the second voyage.

2. *Haec* is needed to identify the goat (cf. μέ in Crinagoras's poem on Augustus's goat in the *Greek Anthology* 9.224 and Pope's "I am his Highness' dog at Kew"). The reward would be that mentioned in the *Anecdotes:* "[She] was then, by the humanity of her amiable master, turned out to graze in Kent, as *a recompence* (my italics) for her utility and faithful service" (O.183). It is arguably a defect that the reward is not made clear in the poem itself. **2.** Jove's nurse was the goat Amalthea (Aratus, *Phaenomena* 163, Callimachus, *Hymns* 1.47–48 etc.).

O.188–90, Y.271–73, B.75–76

Γνῶθι σεαυτόν

(*Post Lexicon Anglicanum auctum et emendatum*)

Lexicon ad finem longo luctamine tandem
Scaliger ut duxit, tenuis pertaesus opellae,
Vile indignatus studium, nugasque molestas,
Ingemit exosus, scribendaque lexica mandat
Damnatis, poenam pro poenis omnibus unam.
  Ille quidem recte, sublimis, doctus, et acer,
Quem decuit majora sequi, majoribus aptum,
Qui veterum modo facta ducum, modo carmina vatum,
Gesserat et quicquid virtus, sapientia quicquid
Dixerat, imperiique vices, coelique meatus,
Ingentemque animo seclorum volverat orbem.
  Fallimur exemplis; temere sibi turba scholarum
Ima tuas credit permitti, Scaliger, iras.
Quisque suum norit modulum; tibi, prime virorum,

Ut studiis sperem, aut ausim par esse querelis,
Non mihi sorte datum, lenti seu sanguinis obsint
Frigora, seu nimium longo jacuisse veterno,
Sive mihi mentem dederit natura minorem.
Te sterili functum cura, vocumque salebris
Tuto eluctatum spatiis sapientia dia
Excipit aethereis, ars omnis plaudit amica,
Linguarumque omni terra discordia concors
Multiplici reducem circumsonat ore magistrum.
Me, pensi immunis cum jam mihi reddor, inertis
Desidiae sors dura manet, graviorque labore
Tristis et atra quies, et tardae taedia vitae.
Nascuntur curis curae, vexatque dolorum
Importuna cohors, vacuae mala somnia mentis.
Nunc clamosa juvant nocturnae gaudia mensae,
Nunc loca sola placent, frustra te, somne, recumbens
Alme voco, impatiens noctis metuensque diei.
Omnia percurro trepidus, circum omnia lustro,
Si qua usquam pateat melioris semita vitae,
Nec quid agam invenio; meditatus grandia, cogor
Notior ipse mihi fieri, incultumque fateri
Pectus, et ingenium vano se robore jactans.
Ingenium, nisi materiem doctrina ministret,
Cessat inops rerum, ut torpet, si marmoris absit
Copia, Phidiaci foecunda potentia coeli.
Quicquid agam, quocunque ferar, conatibus obstat
Res angusta domi, et macrae penuria mentis.
Non rationis opes animus, nunc parta recensens,
Conspicit aggestas, et se miratur in illis,
Nec sibi de gaza praesens quod postulet usus
Summus adesse jubet celsa dominator ab arce;
Non operum serie, seriem dum computat aevi
Praeteriti, fruitur, laetos aut sumit honores
Ipse sui judex, actae bene munera vitae;
Sed sua regna videns, loca nocte silentia late
Horret, ubi vanae species, umbraeque fugaces,
Et rerum volitant rarae per inane figurae.
Quid faciam? tenebrisne pigram damnare senectam
Restat? an accingar studiis gravioribus audax?
Aut, hoc si nimium est, tandem nova lexica poscam?

Know Yourself

(After enlarging and correcting the English Dictionary)

When Scaliger, after a long struggle, finally brought his dictionary to completion, thoroughly fed up with the paltry work, and despising the worthless effort with its boring trivialities, he groaned in disgust, and consigned the writing of dictionaries to the damned as the one punishment that would suffice for all the others.

Quite right he was, that high-minded, learned, and acute man; he should have followed higher aims, for he was fit for greater things. He had handled at one time the feats of ancient generals, at another the songs of poets, and whatever virtue, whatever wisdom had spoken, and he had turned over in his mind the rise and fall of empires, the movements of the firmament, and the mighty cycle of the ages. We are misled by models. The lowest gang of scholars rashly assume that they are entitled to feel your anger, Scaliger. Everyone should know his own limitations. It was not granted to me by my lot that I might aspire to equal your scholarship, preeminent as you are, or claim to share your grievances, whether because the coldness of my sluggish circulation prevents me, or the fact that I have lain too long in a torpor, or because nature has given me an inferior intellect.

Once you had finished the futile task that occupied your mind, and had struggled safely out of the rough pathways of words, divine wisdom welcomed you to the clear expanses of the sky; every art gave you friendly applause, and in every land the discordant tongues, speaking in harmony, sounded with countless voices around the master who had returned.

As for me, now that I am restored to myself, having discharged my duty, the harsh lot of sluggish indolence awaits me, or a black and gloomy leisure that is worse than labor, and the tedium of a slowly passing life. Worries beget worries; a persistent troop of troubles plagues me, the evil dreams of an empty mind. Now I enjoy the rowdy pleasures of a late-night supper, now I delight in lonely places; as I lie in bed, I call in vain to you, kindly sleep, finding the night unbearable and the day terrifying. In fear I run over every possibility, go round everything in the hope of finding if anywhere the path lies open to a better life. Yet I do not discover what to do; after making ambitious plans I am forced to become better known to myself, to admit to having an uncultivated heart and a mind that vainly boasts of its powers. Unless learning gives it material, the mind ceases to work, destitute of subjects, just as, when no marble is available, the creative power of Phidias's chisel is numbed. Whatever I do, wherever I am taken, my efforts are thwarted **(40)** by the straitened circumstances of my home and the poverty of my meager intelligence.

The mind, as it now counts up its gains, does not gaze at the accumulated riches of reason and see itself reflected in them. Nor does the highest controller from his lofty stronghold **(45)** order to be made available to him from his treasures what the present need requires; his own judge, when he reckons up the roll of time past, he takes no pleasure in the roll of his achievements, nor does he joyfully accept honors, the rewards of a well-spent life; but as he contemplates his kingdom he shudders at the silent regions stretching far and wide in the darkness, where insubstantial shapes, fleeting shadows **(50),** and flimsy shapes of things flit through the void.

What shall I do? Is the only course left to condemn my sluggish old age to darkness? Or shall I bravely gird myself for more serious studies? Or if that is too much, shall I end up by demanding another dictionary to work on?

The poem was written after finishing the fourth edition of the *Dictionary* in December 1772. The title is one of the two most famous maxims carved on Apollo's temple at Delphi, the other being "Nothing too much."

Whitman's excuse for his own contradictions: "I am large, I contain multitudes" could have been made with even greater justice by Johnson. Such inclusiveness is seen very clearly in his attitude to dictionaries. In his own work he defines a lexicographer as "a harmless drudge," and at the end of the famous preface he dismisses it "with frigid tranquillity." The same feelings returned as he completed the fourth edition. After starting in a mood of sardonic humor, the poem moves on to a state bordering on mental collapse; then it finishes with another flash of dark humour. Yet Johnson knew very well that the *Dictionary* was a gigantic achievement. And a few months later he was in good spirits (O.187, B.80). Wain's chapters (1980, Chaps. 11, 13, 14) give an excellent account of the whole project.

1–5. Joseph Justus Scaliger (1540–1609) one of the great renaissance polymaths. He wrote the following epigram in his Arabic lexicon: "Anyone who awaits the harsh sentence of a judge in the future, a person who will be condemned to woes and punishments, let him not be worn out by wielding a blacksmith's hammer in prison or have his hands made stiff and painful by mining metal. Let him compile dictionaries; for need I say more? This labour by itself includes every form of punishment." **8–11.** Johnson is referring to Scaliger's works on Thucydides, Polybius, and Caesar (8–9); on Ausonius, Catullus, Tibullus, and Propertius (8–9), on Aristotle and Cicero (9–10), on chronology (*De Emendatione Temporum* and *Thesaurus Temporum*) (10), and on the astronomical poet Manilius (10). The phrase *coelique meatus* (10) occurs in *Aeneid* 6.849, where it refers to the achievements of Greek astronomy. Here, however, it refers to the poem of Manilius. **12.** *Fallimur exemplis* recalls Horace's *decipit exemplar vitiis imitabile* (*Epist.*1.19.17); consciously or otherwise the epistle may have been in his mind after writing *mandat* in v. 4 which echoed Horace's decree, consigning the occupations of law and business to teetotallers (*mandabo siccis* in v. 9). **14.** Literally, everyone should be aware of his own measure. The thought (including *modulus*) comes from Horace, *Epistles* 1.7.98; cf. *Ars Poetica* 39–40 (with a different image). **16–17.** In *Georgics* 2.475ff. Virgil says he would like above all to write about natural phenomena, as Lucretius had done, but if he is prevented from doing so by the cold blood around his heart ("frigidus . . . circum praecordia sanguis" in v. 484), he will write about the countryside. According to Empedocles (Freeman 1956, 63), blood around the heart was the seat of thought and sensation (and hence of poetic ability). **20.** B refers *sapientia dia* to Horace, *Serm.*1.2.32, but the phrase used there is *sententia dia.* Johnson's phrase is rather a variation of *caelestis sapientia* (*Epistles* 1.3.27). **22.** Manilius, *Astronomica* 1.142 had already reversed Horace's *concordia discors* (*Epist.*1.12.19). Johnson uses the phrase again in connection with the metaphysical poets in *The Life of Cowley.* **23–51.**The terrible and convincing picture of Johnson's mental state might seem to have nothing in common with Horace's experience. But that is because the conventional picture of the cheerful, well-adjusted Roman poet is far from complete. Leaving aside the melancholy of some of the greatest odes (e.g., 1.4 ad fin., 2.3 ad fin. 2.14, 4.7), I quote only *Epist.*1.8.3–11:

> If he asks how I am, tell him that in spite of good resolutions
> my life is neither right nor pleasant; not because hail
> has beaten down my vines, or heat has blighted my olives,
> nor because herds of mine are sick on a distant pasture,
> but because, while I'm physically fit, I'm mentally ill.
> And yet I don't want to hear or know about possible treatments.
> I'm rude to the doctors who wish me well, and can't think why
> my friends are fussing to rid me of this accursed depression.
> I go for things that are bad for me, and avoid what I think would help.

23. *Reducem* seems to have the second sense given by *Ox.Lat.Dict.,* i.e., "returned"; Scaliger has done with his useless lexicography and is welcomed back by philosophy and the arts. The idea is then taken up by Johnson, who is now restored to himself (24), cf. Horace (*Epist.*1.14.1) of his rural retreat "which restores me to myself" (mihi me reddentis agelli). **26.** Eichholz, cited in Tucker and Gifford (1957) 218 n. 3, suggests that "tristis et atra quies" is an ironic echo of Virgil's "dulcis et alta quies" (*Aen.*6.522). **40–41.** "Obstat / res angusta domi" is from Juvenal 3.164–65, cf. *London* 177. **43.** "se miratur in illis": literally "admires itself in them"; I have given what I think Johnson meant. **45.** The line recalls Statius, *Silv.*2.2.131 "celsa tu mentis ab arce," which makes it clear that the *dominator* is the reason. The idea goes back to Plato; cf. *Republic* 4.441–42. **46–7.** The traditional text has "Non operum serie, seriem dum computat aevi, / Praeteritis fruitur". It is objectionable to give *fruitur* two objects (*serie* and *praeteritis*). I have therefore repunctuated and emended as above; cf. O.198, *The Fly,* v. 11, "praeteritae numeranti tempora vitae," and 240, *Prayer* 6.5 "lapsi quem poenitet aevi." **49.** B notes the precedents in Virgil, *Ecl.*1.69 and *Aen.*6.265. **50.** Horace, *Ars Poetica* 6–7 speaks of *vanae species* (fantastic iamages) "velut aegri somnia" (like an invalid's dreams). **51.** The void (*inane*) is one of the two central concepts in Lucretius's physics, the other being atoms. In book 4 Lucretius describes the images that cause terror to the sleeper: "membranae . . . volitant ultroque citroque per auras" (31–32) (films . . . flit hither and thither through the air); also "dico igitur rerum effigies tenuisque figuras / mittier ab rebus summo de corpore eorum" (51–52) (I say, then, that images and flimsy shapes of things are thrown from their outer surface). **54.** Johnson seems to have extended the usual sense of *posco.* He is clearly not demanding another dictionary from somebody else. The nearest case I can think of is Horace, *Serm.*2.3.2, where it is used of calling for parchment with the intention of working on it. Johnson ends with a sardonic joke against himself, recalling the opening reference to Scaliger.

David Venturo says of this poem "Johnson relies on a nexus of allusions to Virgil's *Aeneid* to create a playfully mocking contrast between the tribulations of the epic hero, Aeneas, and the Johnsonian anti-hero" (2000, 33, 2, 71). Before accepting this interesting idea one needs to know what the nexus of allusions consists of. Referring back to his earlier book (1999, 141–43) one finds the same suggestion; but it is doubtful if the passages cited there are numerous and specific enough to support the thesis; *Aen.*2.564 ("respicio et, quae sit me circum copia, lustro") is compared with Johnson's v. 32 ("omnia percurro trepidus, circum omnia lustro"), and *Aen.*6.263 ("ille ducem haud timidis vadentem passibus aequat") is thought to be echoed, by way of a mocking contrast, by the word *horret* in Johnson v. 50. If we are being invited to see Johnson's sufferings as in some way parallel to those of Aeneas, this would have to be established more precisely. In the meantime it is safer simply to recall that Johnson's poem is written in hexameters throughout, and all the references I have noted are to hexametric poems. The effect is therefore more weighty than in the case of elegiacs, whether Johson is being simply serious, or whether, as in the opening and at the end, he is being satirically serious.

O.190, Y.275–76, B.86–87

Verses Addressed to Dr Lawrence, Composed by Dr Johnson, as He Lay Confined with an Inflamed Eye

Sanguine dum tumido suffusus flagrat ocellus,
Deliciasque fugit solitas solitosque labores;

Damnatus tenebris, lectoque affixus inerti,
Quid mecum peragam, quod tu doctissime posses
Laurenti saltem facili dignarier aure?
Humanae mentis, rerum se pascere formis,
Est proprium, et quavis captare indagine verum
Omnibus unus amor, non est modus unus amoris.
Sunt qui curriculo timidi versantur in arcto,
Quos soli ducunt sensus, solus docet usus;
Qui sibi sat sapiunt, contenti noscere quantum
Vel digiti tractant, oculus vel sentit et auris:
Tantundem est illis, repleat spatia ardua coeli
Materies, vastum an late pandatur inane.
Scire vices ponti facile est, nil amplius optant
Nec quaerunt quid, luna, tuo cum fluctibus orbi.
Sic sibi diffisi, lenta experientia cursum
Qua sulcat, reptant tuti per lubrica vitae.
Altera pars hominum, sanctae rationis alumni,
Permissum credit nudas sibi sistere causas,
Materiemque rudem, magnaeque parentis adesse
Conciliis, verique sacros recludere fontes.
Gens illa, impatiens per singula quaeque vagandi
Tentat iter brevius, magno conamine summam
Naturae invadens, mundique elementa refingens
Laevia serratis miscens, quadrata rotundis,
Corpora cuncta suis gestit variare figuris,
Particulasque locans, certas certo ordine, pulchram
Compagem edificat, coelorum atque aetheris ignes
Accendit, rerumque modos ac foedera ponit.
Hi sunt quos animi generosa insania magni
In sublime rapit, queis terra et pontus et aer
Sub pedibus subjecta jacent; queis ultima primis
Nexa patent; hi sunt quos nil mirabile turbat,
Nil movet insolitum, sub legibus omnia fictis
Dum statuunt, causisque audent prefigere metam.

While my poor eye is inflamed, suffused with swollen blood, shying away from its customary pleasures and customary tasks, while I am condemned to darkness and tied to an inactive bed, what shall I compose from my own resources that you at least, my most learned Lawrence, may be able to judge worthy of your ready ear? **(5)** It is the peculiar characteristic of the human mind to nourish itself on the appearances of things, and everyone shares the desire (though not the same *kind* of desire) to capture the truth in some sort of net. There are those who timidly go round a confined circuit, who are guided by their senses alone and are taught solely by experience **(10).** They know all they want to know, content to understand as much as their fingers handle or their eyes or ears can sense. For them it is all the same whether the lofty spaces of the sky are filled with matter or whether a huge void extends far and wide. It is easy to recognize the sea's tides; they want nothing more **(15),** and do not wish to find out what your orb, o moon, has to do with the waves. Hence, without any self-assurance, they crawl securely through the dubious areas of life, confining themselves to those places where dull experience plows a furrow.

The other part of mankind, the children of holy reason, believe they are entitled to lay bare the causes of things **(20)** and the raw material of which they are made, to be present at the councils of the great parent, and to reveal the sacred springs of truth. Those folk, too impatient to wander through every detail, try a shorter route, breaking in on the totality of nature with a huge effort. Reshaping the elements of the world **(25),** mixing jagged with smooth and square with round, they are eager to change all material things into shapes of their own devising. Putting every piece in its place in a fixed order they build up a fine structure, kindle the fires of the sky and upper air, and fix the boundaries and laws of the universe **(30).** These are the men who are swept aloft by the noble frenzy of their mighty intellect, under whose feet earth, sea, and air lie vanquished, and to whom the connections between all things from first to last are revealed. These are the men who are not unsettled by anything surprising, never disturbed by anything unusual, while they proceed to arrange everything under unchangeable laws **(35)** and have the courage to fix an end to the chain of causation.

The first category of people is easy enough to identify—those who rely on the world of sense perception and do not venture to speculate further. They observe the movement of the tides, but are not interested in finding out how they are related to the moon. On reading v. 11, one may be reminded of the smelly centurion in Persius 3.77ff., who proclaims "quod sapio satis est mihi" and goes on to express his contempt for philosophers, specifically Arcesilaus, who in the third century BC introduced skepticism into the Academy, and also an unnamed physicist, a sick old man, who affirmed the principle "nothing can come from nothing, nothing can pass away into nothing." This is almost certainly Epicurus.

The second category is less clear, because Johnson has named no names. In 14–15 he may intend to distinguish the Epicureans, who thought that the universe, consisting of combinations of atoms and void, was infinite (Bailey 1926, 20–25), from the Stoics, who thought that the spherical world was surrounded by infinite void (Diogenes Laertius, 7.170). The rest contains a few expressions that might include the Stoics, e.g. "aetheris ignes" (29), "nil mirabile turbat" (34), and "sub legibus omnia fictis / Dum statuunt." But there are more echoes of the Epicureans, in particular Lucretius; thus "sistere causas" (20), "recludere fontes" (22), and "sub pedibus subjecta" (33) come from him via Virgil, *Georgics* 2.490 "cognoscere causas," 175 "recludere fontes," and 491 "subiecit pedibus." More directly one can point to "materiem" (21), "summam" (24), "elementa" (25), "corpora" (27), "particulas" (28), "pedibus subjecta" (33), which all occur in *De Rerum Natura;* finally, "quos nil mirabile turbat / Nil movet insolitum" (34–35) also suits the Epicurean ideal of imperturbability. In addition, one would expect such ideas to have some contemporary relevance. And of course atomism was still highly topical in the seventeenth and eighteenth centuries. Gassendi had made the theory acceptable by contending that God, as the first cause, had set the whole scheme in motion; Charleton and others took up this idea in England; Boyle, the experimentalist, in one passage advances the hypothesis that the corpuscles of niter may be like little prisms, "if these little prisms be by a violent heat split . . . they may come to have parts so much smaller than before, and endowed with such sharp sides and angles that, being dissolved . . . their smallness may give them great access to the pores [of the tongue], and the sharpness of their sides and points may fit them to stab and cut." Johnson may have read some similar description of atoms when he speaks of "smooth being mixed with jagged" (26). Atoms also played an important part in the development of Newton's *Principia.* My colleague, Dr. Andrew Pyle, however, points out that the method of the thinker who, impatient of detail, goes straight to nature as a whole (23–25), sounds more like the a priori approach of the rationalist Descartes—cf. "sanctae rationis alumni" in 19. If that is so, perhaps Johnson is making an ironical reference to *all* those thinkers who claimed to understand the physical universe. But I am not qualified to suggest anything more definite on the matter.

Among other reminiscences it is worth mentioning: **8.** "omnibus unus amor," which recalls Virgil, *Georgics* 3.244 "amor omnibus idem," though Virgil's *amor* is far from intellectual. **9.** "sunt qui curriculo etc.," a clever adaptation of Horace, *Odes* 1.1.3, where the phrase refers to charioteers. **26.** In *Epistles* 1.1.100 Horace uses "mutat quadrata rotundis" (changes square to round) to describe his mental and emotional confusion. Johnson's application of that striking expression shows how freely he could transform the "source-material" that he had in his head. **35.** *fictis* is from *figo,* "I fix." **36.** The chain of causes, when traced backward, stops at God.

O.192, Y.277, B.91

On Recovering the Use of his Eyes

Vitae qui varias vices
Rerum perpetuus temperat arbiter,
Laeto cedere lumini
Noctis tristitiam qui gelidae jubet,
Acri sanguine turgidos
Obductosque oculos nubibus humidis
Sanari voluit meos,
Et me, cuncta beans cui nocuit dies
Luci reddidit et mihi.
Qua te laude, Deus, qua prece prosequar?
Sacri discipulus Libri
Te semper studiis utilibus colam.
Grates, summe Pater, tuis
Recte qui fruitur muneribus, dedit.

Eternal governor of the universe, who dost control the varying phases of life, who biddest the gloom of chilly night give way to the joyful light of day, who hast consented that my eyes that were swollen with aching blood and obscured with cloudy moisture should be healed, and restored me, who was hurt by the day that gladdens everything, to the light and to myself—with what praise, o God, with what prayer shall I honor thee? As a disciple of the Holy Bible I will always worship thee with profitable studies. One who makes proper use of thy gifts, Almighty Father, (thereby) offers thanks.

The meter consists of Glyconics — — — ∪∪ — ∪ ⏓ alternating with lesser Asclepiads — — — ∪∪ — — ∪∪ — ∪ ⏓ another Horatian scheme.

Horace at various times shows his awareness of the "varying phases" of human life; the nearest parallel to Johnson (1–2) is *Epod.* 13.7–8 where, after describing a violent storm, he says "deus haec fortasse benigna / reducet in sedem vice" (God will perhaps bring these conditions round again to peace with a benign alternation). He also uses *temperare* twenty-odd times on different occasions. The most relevant case is *Odes* 1.12.13–16 of Jupiter: "quid prius dicam solitis parentis / laudibus, qui res hominum ac deorum, / qui mare ac terras variisque mundum / temperat horis?" (What shall I utter before the customary praises of our Father, who controls the affairs of gods and men, and also sea, land, and sky by changing the seasons?).

7. God consented that Johnson's eye should be healed; the implication, I take it, is that Dr Lawrence performed the actual healing. **8–9.** Cf. Γνῶθι σεαμτόν 24. **12.** *Colam* is best taken as a future indicative, answering the question "With what prayer?" "Profitable," i.e., morally and spiritually profitable to himself and others. **13–14.** The generalization follows on the prayer. The perfect indicative (*dedit*) often has that function. On "recte fruitur" B quotes *Epist.*1.12.2 "si recte frueris".

O.193, Y.278–79, B.97

Skia

Ponti profundis clausa recessibus,
Strepens procellis, rupibus obsita,
Quam grata defesso virentem
Skia sinum nebulosa pandis!

His cura credo sedibus exulat;
His blanda certe pax habitat locis:
Non ira, non moeror quietis
Insidias meditatur horis.

At non cavata rupe latescere,
Menti nec aegrae montibus aviis
Prodest vagari, nec frementes
E scopulo numerare fluctus.

Humana virtus non sibi sufficit,
Datur nec aequum cuique animum sibi
Parare posse, ut Stoicorum
Secta *crepat* nimis alta fallax.

Exaestuantis pectoris impetum,
Rex summe, solus tu regis arbiter,
Mentisque, te tollente, surgunt,
Te recidunt moderante fluctus.

Skye

Closed in by the deep recesses of the ocean, howling with gales, hemmed in by rocks, how welcome a sight you are, misty Skye, as you open your green bay to the weary traveller! From this haven worry, I do believe, is banished; certainly a delightful peace dwells in this place. No anger, no grief devises an attack against its quiet hours. For the sick mind, however, it is of no avail to hide in hollow caves, nor to wander over pathless mountains, nor to count the roaring waves from a cliff. Human virtue is not sufficient unto itself; nor is every person granted the ability to obtain for himself a calm mind, as the overweening Stoic sect falsely babbles. Almighty King, thou alone art the judge that governs the impulse of our turbulent hearts; the waves of our mind mount up when raised by thee, and sink down when thou dost still them.

Written, like the ode to Urbanus, in Alcaics. The sentiments are very Horatian, In *Epist.* 1.11 the poet thinks how pleasant it would be to sit on the shore at Lebedos, a little town in Asia minor, watching the stormy sea (10); but later he says "If it's true that worry is banished by reason and wisdom, / not by a place which commands (*arbiter*) a wide expanse of sea, / emigrants only change their scenery, not their outlook" (26–27). *Epist.* 1.18.112 is even more relevant; there Horace asks Jove simply for life and adequate means: "aequum mi animum ipse parabo" (On my own I'll provide a balanced mind for myself); for parallels see Nisbet and Hubbard (1978) on *Odes* 2.3.1.Where Johnson differs is in the belief that peace of mind cannot be secured by philosophy. To both poets, however, such peace is precarious. See further on 13–16 below and on *The Island of St. Kenneth,* 21.

This poem and the next two present different reactions to the Hebrides. For a fuller picture see Johnson, *A Tour to the Hebrides* and Boswell, *Journal of a Tour to the Hebrides* (Chapman 1961). In the second work (265) we hear how, in the rough crossing from Scalpa to Rasay, Johnson quoted Horace's ode (2.16) beginning "Otium divos rogat in patenti / Prensus Aegaeo" (The man who is caught in the open Aegean prays to the gods for a quiet life).

4. *Sinum* means both "bay" and "bosom." **5.** Horace's image of Black Care sitting behind the horseman (*Odes* 3.1.40) was all too familiar to Johnson. **11–12.** See the note on *Epist.* 1.11 above. **13–16.** *Virtus* was a quality central to Stoic ethics. Speaking of Zeno, Diogenes Laertius says "Virtue, he holds, is a harmonious disposition, to be chosen for its own sake and not from hope or fear or any other motive. Moreover, virtue is that in which happiness consists; for virtue is the state of mind which tends to make the whole of life harmonious" (7.89). The idea of emotional balance or tranquillity (14–15) was common to several schools, but *aequanimitas* (calmness of mind in the face of adversity) was particularly associated with the Stoics (Seneca, *Epist. Moral.* 49.10, 66.13), and that is what Johnson has in mind here. He connects it with the ἀπάθεια or "impassivity" of Stoicism, which he regarded as contrary to nature (*Rambler,* Yale edition vol. 3, 174–79, and *Idler* no. 41). It is worth noting that, according to Boswell, in 15–16 Johnson had once written "utcunque jactet / Grandiloquus nimis alta Zeno" (whatever the excessively high-flown boasts of the grandiloquent Zeno); a memory of the subjunctive *jactet* might explain the mistaken *crepet* (16). **16.** *Crepat* (indicative) should be read rather than *crepet* (subjunctive). **17–20.** Impulse is like a stormy sea. The imagery comes from *Odes* 1.3.14–16: "Noti / quo non arbiter Hadriae / maior, tollere seu ponere vult freta" (the South Wind, than whom there is no greater judge over the Adriatic, whether he wishes to raise or calm the waters). But there is a certain lack of symmetry in Johnson's stanza, for while it makes sense to say that God raises the spirits if they are too low, one can hardly talk of him raising the waves of the mind, i.e., causing disturbance.

O.194–95, Y.280–81, B.103

Oda

Permeo terras, ubi nuda rupes
Saxeas miscet nebulis ruinas,
Torva ubi rident steriles coloni
    Rura labores.

Pervagor gentes, hominum ferorum
Vita ubi nullo decorata cultu
Squallet informis, tugurique fumis
    Foeda latescit.

Inter erroris salebrosa longi,
Inter ignotae strepitus loquelae,
Quot modis mecum, quid agat, requiro,
    Thralia dulcis!

Seu viri curas, pia nupta, mulcet,
Seu fovet mater subolem benigna,
Sive cum libris novitate pascit
    Sedula mentem;

Sit memor nostri, fideique merces
Stet fides constans, meritoque blandum
Thraliae discant resonare nomen
    Littora Sciae.

Ode

I am travelling through a country where bare rocks and stony ruins alike are clothed in mists, where the grim countryside mocks the crofter's barren labors. I am wandering through clans where the life of wild men, enhanced by no culture, is marred by squalor and skulks in ugliness behind the smoke of a hovel. Amid the rough surroundings of my long rambles, amid the noisy chatter of a strange language, in how many ways do I ask myself what sweet Thrale is doing! Whether as a devoted wife she soothes the worries of her husband, or whether as a loving mother she looks after her child, or whether with books she diligently feeds her mind with new knowledge, may she think of me, and may her loyalty stand fast, rewarding the loyalty of another, and may the shores of Skye deservedly learn to reecho to the charming name of Thrale.

Written to Mrs. Thrale on Skye on September 6, 1773. Like *In Theatro,* the ode is in the Sapphic meter, which Horace sometimes employed for his lighter poems about women, e.g., 1.22, 1.30, 2.4, 2.8, 4.11.

In *Odes* 1.22 Horace imagines himself in various unpleasant parts of the world, but wherever he is, he will continue to love the sweetly laughing, sweetly talking Lalage. Lines 17–20 run "Pone me pigris *ubi nulla* campis / arbor aestiva recreatur aura, / quod latus mundi *nebulae* malusque / Iuppiter urget" (Put me in a lifeless plain where no tree is refreshed by a summer breeze, a quarter of the world that is hemmed in by mists and an unkindly sky-god). But Johnson's country is not imaginary; he describes with the distaste of a preromantic the rough alien people as well as the rough alien scenery, and the woman he thinks of is a wife, mother, and scholar, a significant figure in the life of London; all she shares with Lalage is her sweetness.

3. *Rident* imports a sardonic note; could it be an unconscious transformation of Horace's *ridentem* (23)? **10.** The unfamiliar language was Erse, a Gaelic dialect spoken by the Highlanders. **11.** It would be wrong to imagine that *quot modis* was simply a substitute for *quotiens* ("how often") dictated by meter. Johnson goes on to specify the different pictures he has of Mrs. Thrale's life. **17–18.** The mutual loyalty no doubt is meant to be understood as the loyalty of friends; for the relationship see Wain (1980, index, 388). **18–20.** The conceit of "the pathetic fallacy" is more associated with pastoral; cf. Virgil, *Eclogues* 4.50–51, 5.25–28, 58–59, 62–63, 8.1–5. But even allowing for Johnson's humour, to send the name "Thrale" echoing along the shores of Skye (if only in the imagination) seems to point to something warmer than friendship.

O. 196, Y.283–4, B. 106

Insula Sancti Kennethi

Parva quidem regio, sed relligione priorum
  Nota, Caledonias panditur inter aquas;
Voce ubi Cennethus populos domuisse feroces
  Dicitur, et vanos dedocuisse deos.
Huc ego delatus placido per coerula cursu
  Scire locum volui quid daret ille novi.
Illic Leniades humili regnabat in aula,
  Leniades magnis nobilitatus avis:
Una duas habuit casa cum genitore puellas,
  Quas Amor undarum fingeret esse deas:
Non tamen inculti gelidis latuere sub antris,
  Accola Danubii qualia saevus habet;
Mollia non deerant vacuae solatia vitae,
  Sive libros poscant otia, sive lyram.
Luxerat ille dies, legis gens docta supernae
  Spes hominum ac curas cum procul esse jubet.
Ponti inter strepitus sacri non munera cultus
  Cessarunt; pietas hic quoque cura fuit:
Quid quod sacrifici versavit femina libros,
  Legitimas faciunt pectora pura preces.
Quo vagor ulterius? quod ubique requiritur hic est;
  Hic secura quies, hic et honestus amor.

The Island of Saint Kenneth

A small place, to be sure, but one famous for the religion of earlier men, lies open amid Caledonian waters, where Saint Kenneth is said to have tamed the savage people by his voice and to have taught them to abandon their false gods. After sailing here in a calm voyage across a blue sea, I wanted to find what new information the place had to offer. There Maclean held sway in a humble palace, Maclean who held a noble rank in virtue of his mighty ancestors. One cottage housed the father along with his two daughters, whom Love might have imagined to be goddesses of the waves. Yet these were no boorish people, lurking in chilly caves like those inhabited by the savage beside the Danube; the soft comforts of a life of leisure were not lacking, whether their hours of ease called for books or for a harp. That day had dawned on which a community well versed in the law of God bids earthly hopes and worries to be gone. Amid the roar of the sea the offices of sacred worship did not cease; here too, religious observance was a matter of importance. What did it matter if a woman turned the priest's pages? It is pure hearts that give legitimacy to prayers. Why should I wander any further? All that is required anywhere is here; here is serene repose, and here is honourable love.

1–4. Saint Kenneth, a sixth-century Irish abbot, played a large part in the conversion of the Picts; he is supposed to have established the ecclesiastical settlement that eventually became St. Andrews. In Ireland he is known as St. Canice; the cathedral of that name in Kilkenny is thought to be the site of his original church. **4.** Though Cicero uses *dedocere* (to unteach), Johnson is probably thinking of Horace, *Odes* 2.2.19–20, where Virtue reeducates the people in their use of moral language. **8.** *Leniades* is Sir Allan McLean. **19.** The Doctor is in generous mood, willing to make allowances for irregularities. **21.** A clear reminiscence of Horace, *Epist.* 1.11.29–30 "quod petis hic est, / est Ulubris, animus si te non deficit aequus" (What you're looking for is here—or at Ulubrae, if you preserve a balanced mind); *Ulubrae* was a ghost town in Latium. At Auchinleck, Boswell's family home, on Nov. 4, 1773, Boswell (Hill and Powell, 5:381) notes "On the front of the house of Auchinleck is this inscription: ('Quod petis' etc. as above)." Boswell's father believed that it was in a man's power to attain a balanced mind; but Johnson owned to him "his persuasion that it was in a great measure constitutional, or the effect of causes which do not depend on ourselves, and that Horace boasts too much when he says 'aequum mi animum ipse parabo" (*Epist.* 1.18.112)." The idea recurs in Juvenal 10.363–64: "monstro quod ipse tibi possis dare" (I am indicating what you can provide for yourself); there, too, Johnson diverges from his original. Cf. the notes on "Skye" above.

O.197–98, Y.283–84, B.109

The Fly, an Anacreontic

By William Oldys, 1732

Busy, curious, thirsty fly!
Drink with me and drink as I:
Freely welcome to my cup,
Couldst thou sip and sip it up:
Make the most of life you may,

Life is short and wears away.
Both alike are mine and thine
Hastening quick to their decline:
Thine's a summer, mine's no more,
Though repeated to threescore.
Threescore summers, when they're gone,
Will appear as short as one!

Seu te saeva sitis, levitas sive improba fecit,
   Musca meae comitem, participemque dapis,
Pone metum, rostrum fidens immitte culullo,
   Nam licet, et toto prolue laeta mero.
Tu quamcunque tibi velox indulserit annus,
   Carpe diem, fugit, heu, non revocanda dies!
Quae nos, blanda comes, quae nos perducat eodem,
   Volvitur hora mihi, volvitur hora tibi!
Una quidem, sic fata volunt, tibi vivitur aestas,
   Eheu, quid decies plus mihi sexta dedit?
Olim praeteritae numeranti tempora vitae,
   Sexaginta annis non minor unus erit.

Whether it is raging thirst or shameless levity, fly, that has made you companion and sharer of my meal, have no fear, dip your proboscis confidently into my cup (for it's all right with me), and enjoy soaking yourself thoroughly in the wine. Whatever kind of day the swift year has granted you, seize it, for the day speeds past and cannot be recalled! The hour, my charming friend, which will eventually escort us to the same place, is rolling by for me, rolling by for you! Yes, one summer of life is allotted to you (such is fate's decree); alas, what more has my sixtieth given me? Some day, to one who is counting up the length of his past life, one year will be no less than sixty.

Title: *Anacreontic* means in the manner of Anacreon (seventh-century Greek lyric poet from Teos). The large collection of *Anacreontea* from widely different periods can be read in Campbell (1988, 162–247). Nos. 15 (to a carrier pigeon, translated by Johnson on O.214–5, Y.297–98) and 34 (to a cicada) are particularly germane. Lucian's "Praise of the Fly" (Oldfather 1913, 82–95) was also probably in Johnson's mind. **6.** *Carpe diem:* Horace's famous phrase comes from *Odes* 1.11.8. **7.** I have inserted a comma after *nos* to show that *blanda comes* is vocative. The subjunctive *perducat* can be defended as denoting result with *volvitur.*

O.198, Y.281, B.112

Epitaph on Goldsmith

Τὸν τάφον εἰσοράας τὸν Ὀλιβαρίοιο, κόνίην
Ἄφροσι μὴ σεμνὴν, Ξεῖνε, πόδεσσι πάτει·
Οἷσι μέμηλε φύσις, μετρων χάρις, ἔργα παλαιῶν,
Κλαίετε ποιητήν, ἱστορικόν, φυσικόν.

You are gazing at the tomb of Oliver; do not trample on the sacred dust with your mindless feet, stranger. All who care about the natural world, the charm of verses, and the deeds of the ancients, lament one who was poet, historian, and natural scientist.

In Johnson's day it was already thought strange that he should commemorate Goldsmith's unimportant histories and his work on *Animated Nature,* while ignoring his achievement as a novelist (*The Vicar of Wakefield*) and playwright (*She Stoops to Conquer*); see Hill and Powell (1934, 3:84 n. 2).

O.199, Y.285, B.113

On the Duke of Marlborough

Τοῖος Ἄρης βροτολοιγὸς ἐνὶ πτολέμοισι μέμηνε,
Καὶ τοῖος Παφίην πλῆξεν ἔρωτι Θεάν.

Like him did Ares, the bane of men, rage in battle; and like him did Ares strike the Paphian Goddess with love.

The duke (1650–1722) was the greatest general of his age; his wife Sarah (1660–1744) was a friend of the queen and a prominent figure in society. **2.** Paphos in Cyprus was a cult center of Aphrodite. According to Langton the couplet is a version of one by the Abbé Salvini:

Haud alio vultu fremuit Mars acer in armis:
Haud alio Cypriam perculit ore Deam.

Johnson has managed to get in the Homeric epithet, and he has changed *ore* (with his looks) to ἔρωτι (love).

O. 208–9, Y.289, B.115 Lines from a song by John Chalkhill printed in Izaak Walton's *The Compleat Angler:*

Or we sometimes pass an hour
Under a green willow,
That defends us from a shower,
Making earth our pillow;
Where we may
Think and pray,
Before death
Stops our breath:
Other joys
Are but toys,
And to be lamented.

Nunc per gramina fusi,
Densa fronde salicti
Dum defenditur imber,
Molles ducimus horas.
Hic, dum debita morti
Paulum vita moratur,
Nunc rescire priora,
Nunc instare futuris,
Nunc summi prece sancta
Patris Numen adire est.
Quicquid quaeritur ultra,
Caeco ducit amore,
Vel spe ludit inani,
Luctus mox pariturum.

Now stretched out on the grass, with the thick foliage of a willow keeping off the rain, we pass the idle hours. Here, while life pauses a little on its inevitable way towards death, it is possible now to reminisce about the past, now to think ahead into the future, now to approach the spirit of our highest Father in solemn prayer. Any further goal leads a man in blind desire, or else deceives him with vain hopes and before long brings forth grief.

Walton's *Compleat Angler* (1653) had been greatly expanded by the 5th edition, 1676. Johnson has cast his translation in a series of Pherecratics (— — — ∪∪ — ⏓), a line that occurs in many Horatian stanzas, but not on its own. In his version of Chalkhill's song Johnson asks himself what the poet is thinking about, and why joys are to be lamented. After speaking of the right sort of prayer he closes with four lines reminiscent of the *Vanity of Human Wishes.*

7. According to Aulus Gellius 2.19, *rescire* is properly used of finding out something (usually unpleasant) that is hidden or unexpected; however, from his section 4 one infers that it was also used in a less precise sense. One doesn't find out much that is unexpected about the past by lazing under a willow.

O.215–16, Y.298–99, B.117

Ad T.L. M.D.

Fateris ergo quod populus solet
Crepare vaecors, nil sapientiam
  Prodesse vitae, literasque
    In trepidis dare terga rebus.

Tu, queis laborat sors hominum, mala
Nec vincis acer, nec pateris pius;
  Te mille succorum potentem
    Destituit medicina mentis.

Per caeca noctis taedia turbidae,
Pigrae per horas lucis inutiles,
  Torpesque languescisque curis
    Sollicitus nimis, heu! paternis.

Tandem dolori plus satis est datum,
Exsurge fortis, nunc animis opus,
  Te docta, Laurenti, vetustas
    Te medici revocant labores.

Permitte summo res hominum Patri,
Permitte fidens, ac muliebribus
  Amice, majorem querelis,
    Redde tuis, tibi redde, mentem.

So then, you concede what the senseless mob is accustomed to gibber—that wisdom is of no service to life, and that book learning turns tail in moments of crisis. You neither valiantly overcome nor dutifully endure the ills that plague mankind as part of its lot. You, the master of a thousand potions, do not possess a medicine for the mind. Through the dreary darkness of a restless night, through the futile hours of the torpid day you are numb and exhausted, overanxious, alas, with a father's worries. Come now, more than enough has been given to anguish. Stand up, be brave; this is the time for courage! The learning of the ancients, yes and your work as a doctor call you back, Lawrence. Leave men's affairs to the Father in heaven, leave them to him in confidence, and restore to you and yours, my friend, a mind that can rise above womanish wailing.

The poem is written in Alcaics. The title refers to Dr. Thomas Lawrence, who was said to be "a man of strict piety and profound learning" (cf. v. 15 "docta . . . vetustas"); he was thinking with excessive longing of his son, who was living abroad. **14.** At a crucial point in Aeneas's visit to the underworld, the Sibyl says "nunc animis opus, Aenea, nunc pectore firmo" (*Aen.*6.261). **17.** When in *Odes* 1.9.9 Horace says "permitte divis cetera," he means little more than that the balance of nature will reassert itself. Johnson invests the phrase with Christian faith. **18.** In ancient Rome extravagant expressions of grief were expected of women as a social duty. Often mourners were hired for the occasion. When a woman like Cleopatra faced death with fortitude, it was praised as uncharacteristic (Horace, *Odes* 1.37.21–32). Even in the code of eighteenth-century England, too much grief was regarded as unmanly.

O.219, Y.301, B.120

Epilogus

Quae fausta Romae dixit Horatius,
Haec fausta vobis dicimus, Angliae
Opes, triumphos, et subacti
Imperium pelagi precantes.

Epilogue

The blessings that Horace wished for Rome, these blessings we wish for you, praying that England may enjoy prosperity and military triumphs, and that she may rule over the sea which she has subdued.

Johnson's epilogue was written to accompany a musical performance of Horace's *Carmen Saeculare* (Poem for a New Age). The verse is in Alcaics, though the *Carmen Saeculare* itself was in Sapphics. For details of the background see O.218. The cheerful hubris of Arne's "Rule Britannia" had been welcomed in England as long ago as 1740. The sentiment of the present piece, however, was not typical of Johnson, who deprecated imperial expansion and thought that America should be left to the Indians; see his well-known earlier remarks in the *Life of Savage.*

O.223–24, Y.305, B.122

Euripides, Medea. 190–203

Non immerito culpanda venit
Proavum vaecors insipientia,
Qui convivia lautasque dapes
Hilarare suis jussere modis
Cantum, vitae dulce levamen.
At nemo feras iras hominum,
Domibus claris exitiales,
Voce aut fidibus pellere docuit,
Queis tamen aptam ferre medelam
Utile cunctis hoc opus esset,
Namque ubi mensas onerant epulae
Quorsum dulcis luxuria soni?
Sat laetitia, sine subsidiis,
Pectora molli mulcet dubiae
Copia cenae.

Not without justice does the senseless folly of our ancestors incur blame. They decreed that banquets and lavish feasts should be cheered by song, that sweet comforter of life, with its melodies. No one, however, has shown how voice or strings can be employed to banish men's fierce anger, which brings ruin to illustrious families. Yet to devise a suitable medicine for that ill would be a beneficial achievement for everyone. For where tables are loaded with good food, what is the point of the luxury of sweet sound? The abundance of a "doubtful meal" sufficiently gladdens the heart with gentle joy without any additional help.

In Euripides' play these lines are spoken by the nurse to the chorus in lyric meters. Johnson's version is too close to warrant printing the Greek; he gives a fair approximation to the meters.

Partly, perhaps, because Johnson was deaf in the left ear, he admitted to Boswell that he was "very insensible to the power of music." "I once bought a flagelet," he said, "but I never made out a tune" (Hill and Powell 1934, 3.242). Once, after he had responded to Miss Thrale's playing on the harpsichord, Dr. Burney said "I believe we shall make a musician of you at last." Johnson answered, "Sir, I shall be glad to have a new sense given to me" (2.409). Yet even if he had been more receptive, Johnson might not have wished music to interfere with the food and conversation at a dinner party.

5. One suspects that Johnson may have thought first of Horace's *dulce lenimen* [sweet soother] in *Odes* 1.32.15, which does refer to music, and then realized that, as the first *e* of *lenimen* was long, the phrase did not fit his meter. So he turned to Catullus's *dulce levamen* (68.61), which did fit his meter, though it referred to a stream of water. **14–15.** In Terence, *Phormio* 342 "a doubtful meal" is one so lavish that one doesn't know what dish to take for preference.

O.224, Y.305, B.124.

Prayer on Christmas Day, 1779

Nunc dies Christo memoranda nato
Fulsit, in pectus mihi fonte purum
Gaudium sacro fluat, et benigni
    Gratia Coeli!

Christe, da tutam trepido quietem,
Christe, spem praesta stabilem timenti;
Da fidem certam, precibusque fidis
    Annue, Christe.

Now the day that is made memorable by the birth of Christ has dawned; let pure joy from the sacred spring flow into my breast, and the grace of kindly Heaven! Christ, grant me a safe repose when fearful; Christ, vouchsafe me a firm hope when anxious; grant me a sure faith, o Christ, and answer my faithful prayers.

The stanzas are in the Sapphic meter.

O.228, Y.278, B.96

Robin of Doncaster's Epitaph

What I gave that I have;
What I spent that I had;
What I left that I lost.

Ex Anglico

Habeo dedi quod alteri;
Habuique quod dedi mihi;
Sed quod reliqui perdidi.

Johnson has added indirect objects in vv. 1–2, and has contrived internal and final rhymes.

O.229

Chloe

Chloe new marry'd looks on men no more!
Why then, 'tis plain for what she looked before!

Ex Anglico

Nunc nova nupta viros cessat spectare Lycoris;
Nonne ita spectarit cur prius illa docet?

"Chloe" is an epigram by William Walsh, printed in 1692.

1. The opening *num* of the Oxford text makes no sense; *num* and *nunc* are frequently confused; here the error may be partly due to the interrogative *nonne* immediately below. *Nunc* nicely balances *prius*.

O.229, Y.309, B.126

On Mrs. Thrale

Hostem odit tacite, sed amicum ridet aperte
Thralia. Quid mavis? tutius hostis eris.

Thrale gives no sign when she hates a foe, but laughs openly at a friend. Which do you prefer? You'll be more safely placed as a foe.

2. *tutior* would be more common than *tutius.*

O.229, Y.309, B.127

A Summons to Dr Lawrence

Phoebe fave, aegrotat quae te colit, ulla nec usquam est
Quam magis exoptes arte valere tua.

Phoebus, bring help; the lady who reveres you is ill; and there is no woman anywhere whom you would prefer to get well as a result of your skill.

Johnson flatters Lawrence by addressing him as Phoebus, Apollo being the god of healing.

O.230, Y.308, B.125

The Collect for Ash Wednesday

Almighty and everlasting God, who hatest nothing that thou hast made, and dost forgive the sins of all them that are penitent; create and make in us new and contrite hearts, that we, worthily lamenting our sins and acknowledging our wretchedness, may obtain of thee, the God of all mercy, perfect remission and forgiveness, through Jesus Christ our Lord.

Summe Deus, qui semper amas quodcunque creasti,
Judice quo scelerum est poenituisse salus,
Da veteres noxas animo sic flere novato,
Per Christum ut veniam sit reperire mihi.

Almighty God, who dost always love what thou hast made, before whom as judge to have repented of one's sins is salvation, grant that with my soul made new I may so lament my former sins as to be able to obtain forgiveness through Christ.

Johnson has condensed the original without losing very much and has made it a personal prayer.

O.230, Y.309, B.129

Jejunium et cibus

Serviat ut menti corpus jejunia serva,
  Ut mens utatur corpore, sume cibos.

Fasting and Food

That the body may obey the mind, observe a fast; that the mind may make use of the body, take food.

O.231–32, Y.310–11, B.129–30

Nugae anapaesticae in lecto lusae. Medico Aeger S.

Nunc mihi facilis
Liberiori
Cursu spiritus
Itque reditque;
Nunc minus acris
Seu thoracem
Sive abdomen
Laniat tussis;
Tantum prodest
Tempore justo
Secare venam;
Tantum prodest
Potente succo
Dulce papaver.
Quid nunc superest?
Ut modo tentem
Quantum strictam
Mollia laxent
Balnea pellem,
Cras abiturus
Quo revocarit
Thralia suavis.

Hoc quoque superest
Ut tibi, gentis
Medicae princeps,
Habeam grates,
Votaque fundam
Ne, quae prosunt
Omnibus, artes
Domino desint.
Vive valeque.

A Game with Anapaestic Trifles Played in Bed. Patient sends greetings to Doctor.

Now my breathing is easy, coming and going with a freer flow; now my cough tears less roughly at my chest and stomach; such is the benefit of cutting a vein at the right time; such is the benefit of the mild poppy with its powerful juice. What now remains to be done? That I should try just how far gentle baths relax the tight skin; for tomorrow I am due to go to where the charming Thrale has once again invited me. There is also this—that I should express my thanks to you, the foremost member of the medical profession, and offer a prayer that those arts which benefit everyone else may not fail their master. Live long and stay well.

The meter varies; strict anapaests (as in 25–26) are very much in the minority.

2. *Liberiori* is an ablative ending in *-i,* going with *cursu.* **28–30.** It has been observed by T. Kaminski (2002, 222–38) that these lines cleverly reproduce the complaint of *Apollo medicus* as he pursues Daphne in Ovid, *Metamorphoses* 1.523–24: "ei mihi, quod nullis amor est sanabilis herbis / nec prosunt domino, quae prosunt omnibus artes!" (Ah me, that love is not curable by any herbs, and that the arts which help everybody else are of no help to their lord!). **31.** In view of the context I have translated literally, but the words are a conventional formula of leave-taking.

O.236, Y.312, B.133

Christ to the Sinner

Spe non inani confugis,
Peccator, ad latus meum;
Quod poscis, haud unquam tibi
Negabitur solatium.

With no empty hope, sinner, do you take refuge at my side; the comfort that you seek will never be denied you.

The devotional content and the iambic dimeters rhyming a b c b recall Christian hymns; cf. the verse from Prudentius's *Cathemerinon* quoted by Raby (1953, 57)

cum vasta signum buccina
terris cremandis miserit,
et scissus axis cardinem
mundi ruentis solverit.

Many more famous pieces have a different rhyme scheme; e.g., "vexilla regis prodeunt" (89–90), "veni, creator spiritus" (183), "dulcis Iesu memoria" (330).

1. Cf. *The Vanity of Human Wishes* (349–50): "Enquirer, cease, Petitions yet remain, / Which Heav'n may hear, nor deem Religion vain."

O.236, Y.312, B.134

Spes

Hora sic peragit citata cursum
Sic diem sequitur dies fugacem!
Spes novas nova lux parit, secunda
Spondens omnia credulis homullis;
Spes ludit stolidas, metuque caeco
Lux angit miseros cadens homullos.

Hope

Thus the swift hour completes its course; thus one day follows another as it flees! A new dawn brings forth new hopes, promising poor credulous mortals that all will turn out well; it mocks foolish hopes, and, as it fades, the daylight plagues poor wretched mortals with blind fear.

This desolate piece was composed on Ash Wednesday. The eleven-syllable meter, associated above all with Catullus, is unique in Johnson. Perhaps he thought of the mood of those memorable lines in Catullus 5: "soles occidere et redire possunt: / nobis cum semel occidit brevis lux, / nox est perpetua una dormienda" (Suns can go down and return; for us, once our brief sun has gone down, there is one eternal night for sleeping). Other touches are Horatian: e.g., *Odes* 2.18.15–16: "truditur dies die / novaeque pergunt interire lunae" (One day is pushed on by the next, and new moons hurry to their death) and, most famously, *Odes* 2.14.1–2: "Eheu fugaces, Postume, Postume, / labuntur anni" (Alas, Postumus, Postumus, the flying years slip by)—an ode translated by Johnson in his youth (O.11–12). The diminutives *homullis* (4) and *homullos* (6) convey pathos.

O.237, Y.313, B.136

Prayer on Losing the Power of Speech

Summe Pater, quodcunque tuum de corpore Numen
  Hoc statuat, precibus Christus adesse velit:
Ingenio parcas, nec sit mihi culpa rogasse,
  Qua solum potero parte, placere tibi.

Almighty Father, whatever thy holy power may decide about this body, may Christ consent to attend to my prayer: spare my mind, and may it not count as a fault to have asked to please thee with the only part by which I shall be able to do so.

These lines were written in the night of June 16, 1783, when a terrifying stroke deprived the poet temporarily of speech. It is significant of the place that Latin had in Johnson's life that he should choose it to test whether his faculties had been impaired. The ultimate dread recalls: "From Marlborough's eyes the streams of dotage flow, / And Swift expires a driv'ler and a show" (*The Vanity of Human Wishes,* 316–17).

O.237–38, Y.344–45, B.137–38

Christianus Perfectus

Qui cupit in sanctos Christo cogente referri,
Abstergat mundi labem, nec gaudia carnis

Captans, nec fastu tumidus, semperque futuro
Instet, et evellens terroris spicula corde,
Suspiciat tandem clementem in numine Patrem.
Huic quoque, nec genti nec sectae noxius ulli,
Sit sacer orbis amor, miseris qui semper adesse
Gestiat, et, nullo pietatis limite clausus,
Cunctorum ignoscat vitiis, pietate fruatur.
Ardeat huic toto sacer ignis pectore, possit
Ut vitam, poscat si res, impendere vero.
Cura placere Deo sit prima, sit ultima, sanctae
Irruptum vitae cupiat servare tenorem;
Et sibi, delirans quanquam et peccator in horas
Displiceat, servet tutum sub pectore rectum;
Nec natet, et nunc has partes, nunc eligat illas,
Nec dubitet quem dicat herum, sed, totus in uno,
Se fidum addicat Christo, mortalia temnens.
Sed timeat semper, caveatque ante omnia, turbae
Ne stolidae similis leges sibi segreget audax
Quas servare velit, leges quas lentus omittat,
Plenum opus effugiens, aptans juga mollia collo
Sponte sua demens; nihilum decedere summae
Vult Deus, at, qui cuncta dedit tibi, cuncta reposcit.
Denique perpetuo contendit in ardua nisu,
Auxilioque Dei fretus, jam mente serena
Pergit, et imperiis sentit se dulcibus actum.
Paulatim mores, animum, vitamque refingit,
Effigiemque Dei, quantum servare licebit,
Induit, et, terris major, coelestia spirat.

He who desires to be counted among the saints when Christ is bringing them together must wipe away worldly stain; he must not crave the pleasures of the flesh, nor be puffed up with pride, and he must continually press towards the future; plucking out the barbs of fear from his heart, he must at the last look up to the Father who is merciful in his divine power. He must bear malice to no race or religion, cherish a sacred love of the world, eager always to assist the poor; his devotion must not be in any way confined; he must forgive the trespasses of all, and take pleasure in devotion. The holy fire must burn throughout his heart **(10),** so that he may be able, if the situation demands it, to sacrifice his life for the truth.

Let his first and last concern be to please God; let him strive to keep unbroken the tenor of a saintly life; and though he may displease him by going off the rails and sinning from hour to hour, let him preserve within his heart the knowledge of what is right. Let him not waver, choosing now this side, now that, nor hesitate about whom to call "Master," but, wholly committed to one, let him hand himself over to Christ as a faithful servant, despising earthly things.

But let him always be wary, and take care above all else not, like the foolish mob, to make for himself rash distinctions **(20)** between which laws he is prepared to observe and which he may slackly ignore, evading the full commitment, and stupidly fitting a gentle yoke on his neck to suit his own convenience. God wants nothing to fall short of the total sum, but having given everything to you, he demands everything in return.

Finally, in an unending struggle he tramps along the upward path, and relying on God's help he now presses on with a serene mind, and feels himself impelled by welcome orders. Little by little he reforms his habits, his mind, and his life; he puts on the guise of God, in so far as he can keep it in place, and too great for the earth, he breathes the air of heaven **(30).**

Johnson uses didactic hexameters (like those of Virgil's *Georgics*) to present Christian teaching, as Prudentius, Paulinus, Bede, Alcuin and many others had done before him.

4. Horace had "spinas animo . . . evellas" (*Epist.*1.14.4–5); Johnson's variation could be entirely original, but equally he may have remembered it from a Christian source. **9.** The repetition of *pietate* is not good. **14.** "Going off the rails" is colloquial for us, but that is what *delirans* [going off the furrow] originally meant. **23–24.** There may be an allusion to the parable of the talents in Matthew 25:14–30, especially v. 27 "Thou oughtest therefore to have put my money to the exchangers, and then at my coming I should have received mine own with usury."

O.238–40, Y.345–48, B.140–44

Prayers

I

Pater benigne, summa semper lenitas,
Crimine gravatam plurimo mentem leva:
Concede veram poenitentiam, precor,
Concede agendam legibus vitam tuis.
Sacri vagantes luminis gressus face
Rege, et tuere, quae nocent pellens procul;

Veniam petenti, summe da veniam, Pater;
Veniaeque sancta pacis adde gaudia:
Sceleris ut expers omnis, et vacuus metu,
Te mente pura, mente tranquilla, colam:
Mihi dona morte haec impetret Christus sua.

Kindly Father, always gentle in the highest degree, raise up my mind which is weighed down by many many sins; grant me, I pray thee, the gift of true repentance; grant that I may live my life according to thy laws. Guide my wandering steps with the torch of thy holy light, and protect me, driving the things that harm me far away. To one who begs for pardon, grant pardon, o Father on high, and to pardon add the holy joys of peace, so that delivered from all evil, and freed from fear, I may worship thee with a mind both pure and tranquil. May Christ obtain these gifts for me by his death.

The poem is written in iambic trimeters, i.e., three groups of two iambic feet.

It has been suggested that the prayer was inspired by the *Collect for the Third Sunday after Easter,* which runs as follows: "Almighty God, who shewest to them that be in error the light of thy truth, to the intent that they may return into the way of righteousness; grant unto all them that are admitted into the fellowship of Christ's Religion that they may eschew those things that are contrary to their profession, and follow all such things as are agreeable to the same; through our Lord Jesus Christ." The connection, however, seems rather tenuous.

II

Aeterne rerum conditor,
Salutis aeternae dator;
Felicitatis sedibus
Qui nec scelestos exigis,
Quoscumque scelerum poenitet;
Da, Christe, poenitentiam,
Veniamque, Christe, da mihi;
Aegrum trahenti spiritum
Succurre praesens corpori,
Multo gravatam crimine
Mentem benignus alleva.

Eternal creator of the world, giver of eternal salvation, who dost not expel the sinful from the abodes of blessedness if they repent of their sins, grant me penitence, O Christ, and grant me forgiveness; come swiftly with aid to a body that is drawing breath in pain; of thy kindness bring relief to a mind oppressed with a great burden of sin.

1. The line is taken from a poem of St. Ambrose that is printed in Raby (1953, 34). Of this opening linc B says that "both it and the following one look and sound as Horatian as they do Christian"—an observation that I find surprising. The verses are in iambic dimeters.

III

O Qui benignus crimina ignoscis, Pater,
Facilisque semper confitenti ades reo,
Aurem faventem precibus O praebe meis;
Scelerum catena me laborantem gravi
Aeterna tandem liberet clementia,
Ut summa laus sit, summa Christo gloria.

O Father, who in thy mercy dost pardon sins, and art ever ready to succour him who confesseth his guilt, O lend a favourable ear to my supplications; may thy eternal compassion set me free, I beg thee, as I struggle under a heavy chain of sins, so that Christ may enjoy the highest praise, the highest glory.

The ninth of the *Prayers and Thanksgivings upon Several Occasions* may have been in Johnson's mind: "O God, whose nature and property is ever to have mercy and to forgive, receive our humble petitions; and though we be tied and bound with the chain of our sins, yet let the pitifulness of thy great mercy loose us; for the honour of Jesus Christ, our Mediator and Advocate." But, as with the other Collects, Johnson makes it a private prayer.

5. *Tandem* often intensifies appeals; it could have its usual sense of "at the last," but that idea is not present in the English prayer.

IV

Per vitae tenebras rerumque incerta vagantem
   Numine praesenti me tueare Pater!
Me ducat lux sancta, Deus, lux sancta sequatur;
   Usque regat gressus gratia fida meos.
Sic peragam tua jussa libens, accinctus ad omne
   Mandatum, vivam sic moriarque tibi.

As I wander through the darkness of life and the world's uncertainties, protect me, o Father, with thy ever-present power! May thy holy light precede me, o God; may thy holy light follow me, may thy unfailing grace ever guide my footsteps. So shall I gladly carry out thy commands, girt in readiness for every task, so shall I live and die for thee.

1. Cf. *The Vanity of Human Wishes,* 6–10. **3.** It has been pointed out that this line is based on the *Collect for the Seventeenth Sunday after Trinity:* "Lord, we pray thee that thy grace may always prevent [i.e., precede] and follow us." **5–6.** The concluding couplet is much more loosely related to the rest of the Collect: "And make us continually to be given to all good works."

V

Me, Pater omnipotens, de puro respice coelo,
  Quem moestum et timidum crimina dira gravant;
Da veniam pacemque mihi, da mente serena,
  Ut tibi quae placeant, omnia promptus agam.
Solvi, quo Christus cunctis delicta redemit,
  Et pro me pretium tu patiare, Pater.

Almighty Father, from the pure regions of heaven look down upon me, who in fear and wretchedness am weighed down by dreadful sins; grant me pardon and peace; grant that with a quiet mind I may promptly perform thy every wish. Allow that price, through which Christ redeemed the sins of all, to be paid for me too, o Father.

The *Collect for the Twenty-First Sunday after Trinity* runs thus: "Grant, we beseech thee, merciful Lord, to thy faithful people pardon and peace, that they may be cleansed from all their sins, and serve thee with a quiet mind; through Jesus Christ our Lord."

Again, the collective prayer has been transmuted into an urgent personal appeal.

VI

Summe Dator vitae, naturae aeterne Magister,
  Causarum series quo moderante fluit,
Respice quem subigit senium morbique seniles,
  Quem terret vitae meta propinqua suae,

Respice inutiliter lapsi quem poenitet aevi,
   Recte ut poeniteat respice, magne Parens.

O highest giver of life, eternal Lord of nature, under whose control the chain of causes flows, look kindly upon one oppressed by age and the illnesses of age, who is terrified by the fast-approaching end of his life; look kindly on one who is sorry for the time that has so uselessly drifted by; look kindly upon him, great Parent, and make him truly penitent.

The poem was written before dawn on New Year's Day, 1784.

If, as some have thought, the prayer is based on the *Collect for the Second Sunday after Epiphany,* the transformation is complete.

VII

Summe Pater, puro collustra lumine pectus,
   Anxietas noceat ne tenebrosa mihi.
In me sparsa manu virtutum semina larga
   Sic ale, proveniat messis ut ampla boni.
Noctes atque dies animo spes laeta recurset,
   Certa mihi sancto flagret amore fides.
Certa vetet dubitare fides, spes laeta timere,
   Velle vetet cuiquam non bene sanctus amor.
Da, ne sint permissa, Pater, mihi praemia frustra,
   Et colere et leges semper amare tuas.
Haec mihi, quo gentes, quo saecula, Christe, piasti,
   Sanguine, peccanti promereare tuo!

Father in heaven, bathe my heart in pure light lest the dread of darkness should do me harm, and nourish with so generous a hand the seeds of righteousness that have been cast upon me, that an abundant harvest of goodness may come forth. Night and day may a joyful hope keep flooding my mind, may I have a firm faith burning with holy love. May such a firm faith banish doubt, such a joyful hope banish fear, and such holy love banish ill will toward anyone. Grant, o Father, that I may always observe thy laws with love, so that thy gifts may not have been awarded to me in vain. Earn, o Christ, these blessings for me, thy sinner, through the blood with which thou hast redeemed the nations and the ages!

O.241, Y.341, B.146

A Meditation

Mens mea, quid quereris? veniet tibi mollior hora,
  In summo ut videas numine laeta Patrem;
Divinam in sontes iram placavit Jesus;
  Nunc est pro poena poenituisse reis.

My heart, why are you complaining? A gentler hour will come to you, that you may see with joy the Father in his power on high. Jesus has appeased his divine anger against sinners; now for the guilty penitence has taken the place of a penalty.

1. For the mental and emotional content cf. Horace, *Epist.*1.4.12–14: "inter spem curamque, timores inter et iras / omnem crede diem tibi diluxisse supremum: / grata superveniet quae non sperabitur hora" (In a world torn by hope and worry, dread and anger / imagine every day that dawns is the last you'll see; / the hour you never hoped for will bring a happy surprise).

O.169, Y.257, B.68

On Lord Anson

Gratum animum laudo; Qui debuit omnia ventis,
  Quam bene ventorum surgere templa jubet!

I commend a grateful heart; how right that one who owed everything to the winds should have a temple of the winds erected!

With his prize-money Admiral George Anson (1697–1762) bought Moor Park and built a temple of the winds. For his distinguished career see *Ox Dict. Nat. Biog.* 2.260-66.

Translations from the Greek Anthology

O.242ff., Y.316ff., B.203ff. The Greek is cited only when some difference is worthy of comment.

5.67 Capito

Κάλλος ἄνευ χαρίτων τέρπει μόνον, οὐ κατέχει δέ,
 ὡς ἄτερ ἀγκίστρου νηχόμενον δέλεαρ.

Beauty without charm gives pleasure only, but does not hold—like a bait floating without a hook.

Forma animos hominum capit, at, si gratia desit,
 Non tenet; esca natat pulchra, sed hamus abest.

Beauty attracts people's attention, but if charm is absent does not hold it; the pretty bait floats, but there is no hook.

The Greek is more tightly organized, but Johnson has obtained a more punchy effect by leaving out "like" and employing a double antithesis.

5.74 Rufinus

Floribus in pratis legi quos ipse, coronam
 Contextam variis, do, Rhodoclea, tibi:
Hic anemone humet, confert narcissus odores
 Cum violis; spirant lilia mista rosis.
His redimita comas, mores depone superbos:
 Haec peritura nitent; tu peritura nites!

I am giving you, Rhodocle, a garland woven of various flowers that I myself picked in the meadows: here is the moist anemone, the narcissus along with violets contributes scent; lilies mixed with roses breathe fragrance. After binding your hair with all these, put down your haughty attitude. These bloom to die; you bloom to die!

In the last line Rufinus has ἀνθεῖς καὶ λήγεις καὶ σύ καὶ ὁ στέφανος [You bloom and fade—both you and the garland]. Johnson's idea is more artificial; yet it implies that the difference between the girl and the flowers is simply that between *-nt* and *-s*.

6.1 Plato

Illa triumphatrix Graium consueta procorum
Ante suas agmen Lais habere fores,
Hoc Veneri speculum; nolo me cernere qualis
Sum nunc; nec possum cernere qualis eram.

The famous all-conquering Lais, who was used to having a troop of Greek lovers outside her door, (dedicates) this mirror to Venus; I refuse to see myself as I now am, and cannot see myself as I was.

Johnson has substituted *triumphatrix* for Plato's Ἡ σοβαρὸν γελάσασα καθ' Ἑλλάδος (Who laughed scornfully at Greece).

7.128 Anon.

Heraclitus ego; indoctae ne laedite linguae,
Subtile ingenium quaero, capaxque mei,
Unus homo mihi pro sexcentis, turba popelli
Pro nullo, clamo nunc tumulatus idem.

I am Heraclitus; you ignorant tongues, do not annoy me! I am looking for a subtle intelligence, capable of understanding me; one *man* in my eyes is worth six hundred , the swarming rabble worth nothing. I proclaim this now from my grave.

The Greek ending is more impressive: ταῦτ' αὐδῶ καὶ παρὰ Περσεφόνῃ (I proclaim this even in the house of Persephone).

7.136 Antipater

Exiguum en! Priami monumentum; haud ille meretur
Quale, sed hostiles quale dedere manus.

See, the paltry grave of Priam; he does not deserve such, but such did the enemies' hands give him.

In Antipater the grave speaks in the first person. Both writers will have recalled that in the first instance Priam's headless corpse is left lying on the shore (*Aeneid* 2.557–58).

7.151 Anon

Hector dat gladium Ajaci, dat balteum et Ajax
Hectori, at exitio munus utrique fuit.

Hector gives his sword to Ajax., and Ajax gives his belt to Hector, but the gift was fatal to each.

The next epigram (152) explains that Ajax killed himself with Hector's sword, and Hector was dragged around Troy by Ajax's belt. Johnson contrives a neat chiasmus—Hector-Ajax—Ajax-Hector.

7.239 Parmenio

Funus Alexandri mentitur fama; fidesque
si Phoebo, victor nescit obire diem.

The report of Alexander's death is false; if Phoebus can be relied on, the victorious one cannot die.

Apollo's priestess had proclaimed him invincible (Plutarch, *Alex.* 14.4); if that was true, he should not have been conquered by Hades.

7.265 Plato

Naufragus hic jaceo; contra jacet ecce colonus!
Idem Orcus terrae, sic, pelagoque subest.

I am the grave of a shipwrecked sailor; the one opposite is that of a farmer. So Death lurks alike on land and sea.

The epigrams that appear in the anthology under the name of Plato were not written by the philosopher; see Page (1981, 125–27).

7.282 Theodoridas

Naufragus hic jaceo; fidens tamen utere velis,
Tutum aliis aequor, me pereunte, fuit.

I lie here, a shipwrecked sailor; but set sail in good heart. The sea was safe for others when I perished.

7.284 Asclepiades

Ut vis, ponte minax, modo tres discesseris ulnas,
Ingemina fluctus, ingeminaque sonum.
Si forsan tumulum quo conditur Eumarus aufers,
Nil lucri facies; ossa habet et cinerem.

Provided you keep three arms' lengths away, o threatening sea, redouble your waves as you please, and redouble your roars. If by chance you carry away the mound in which Eumarus is buried, you will make no profit; it contains bones and ashes.

7.318 Callimachus

Quid salvere jubes me, pessime? Corripe gressus;
Est mihi quod non te rideo, plena salus.

Why do you wish me "All the best," you villain? Be off! I enjoy absolutely "all the best" in not having you to laugh at.

2. *rideo* is unsatisfactory, but it may well be that Johnson read the variant γελᾶν (to laugh); modern texts have the superior reading πελᾶν (in not having you near).

7.319 Anon

Et ferus est Timon sub terris; janitor Orci,
Cerbere, te morsu ne petat ille, cave.

Timon is savage even in the underworld; you, Cerberus, Pluto's doorman, take care he doesn't take a bite out of you!

7.350 Anon

Nauta, quis hoc jaceat ne percontere sepulchro;
Eveniat tantum mitior unda tibi!

Sailor, do not ask who lies in this grave; I just hope the wave proves more kindly to you.

7.459 Callimachus

Crethida fabellas dulces garrire peritam
Prosequitur lacrymis filia moesta Sami,
Blandam lanifici sociam, sine fine loquacem,
Quam tenet hic, cunctas quae manet, alta quies.

Crethis was clever at rattling off charming stories. The sad daughters of Samos weep as their thoughts go with her. She was a delightful companion in their wool making, a never-ending chatterer; here she is held fast by that deep quietness that awaits all girls.

1. In *Serm.*2.6.77–78, Horace mentions his country neighbor, Cervius, who would rattle off stories ("garrit . . . fabellas"). **2.** In writing "prosequitur lacrimis" Johnson is thinking of Aeneas in the underworld as he watches Dido disappearing for the last time—an intensely poignant moment (*Aeneid* 6.476). In the attempt to bring out the meaning of *prosequitur* I have had to sacrifice the syntactical unity of the epigram. **4.** Callimachus has ὕπνον (sleep). Johnson cleverly chooses a word that can mean both sleep (as in *Aeneid* 6.522) and silence (as in Statius, *Thebaid* 1.211).

7.461 Meleager

Παμμῆτορ γῆ, χαῖρε· σὺ τὸν πάρος οὐ βαρὺν εἰς σὲ
Αἰσιγένην καὐτὴ νῦν ἐπέχοις ἀβαρής.

Hail, Earth, Mother of all; Aisigenes in the past was not heavy on you; so you should now hold him lightly in your grip.

Cunctiparens Tellus, salve, levis esto pusillo
Lysigeni, fuerat non gravis ille tibi.

Hail, Earth, Mother of all; rest light on little Lysigenes; he was not heavy on you.

Johnson has effectively reversed the order of the prayer and the reason for it; he has economically supplied the idea of "pastness" by using the pluperfect instead of a separate word (πάρος), and by omitting "earth's grip" he has provided a straightforward antithesis of light/heavy. For the wide occurrence of the formula see Lattimore (1962, 65–71).

7.471 Callimachus

Ambraciota, "vale lux alma," Cleombrotus infit,
Et saltu e muro Ditis opaca petit:
Triste nihil passus, animi at de sorte Platonis
Scripta legens, sola vivere mente cupit.

Cleombrotus the Ambracian said "O kindly light, farewell!," and he leaped from a wall, making for the dark regions of Dis: He had suffered nothing tragic, but on reading Plato's work on the fate of the soul, he was eager to live by the mind alone.

Johnson brings out the antithesis light/dark more strongly than Callimachus does, and he adds the last few words of explanation, where Callimachus leaves the motive to be inferred. The work in question is Plato's *Phaedo.*

7.538 Anyte

Μάνης οὗτος ἀνὴρ ἦν ζῶν ποτέ· νῦν δὲ τεθνηκὼς
ἶσον Δαρείῳ τῷ μεγάλῳ δύναται.

Qui jacet hic, *Davus* vixit, nunc, lumine cassus,
Dario magno non minus ille potest.

The man who lies here was Davus in life; now bereft of the light he has no less power than Darius the Great.

The standard text in v. 1 reads "servus vixit"; but Anyte gives the Greek slave's name (*Manes*). One would like to think that in translating the Greek Johnson was equally specific, cf. 7.676 below. A reader, reasonably, reminds me of the principle of generality (not numbering the streaks of the tulip); but that was not Anyte's principle; and in any case it is not clear why Johnson should have acknowledged it in his pentameter and not in his hexameter. So, perhaps rashly, I have supplied *Davus* as a typical slave's name, used by Horace; this provides a satisfactory contrast with *Dario.* If we were dealing with a classical text, the assumption would be that *servus* had been written above *Davus* as an explanatory gloss and was then mistaken for a correction.

Also on **O.91, Y.69, B.60**

7. 553 Damascius

Zosima, quae solo fuit olim corpore serva,
Corpore nunc etiam libera facta fuit.

Zosima, who once was a slave in body only, has now become free of her body as well.

7.560 Paulus Silentiarius

Saepe tuum in tumulum lacrymarum decidit imber
Quem fundit blando junctus amore dolor;
Charus enim cunctis, tanquam, dum vita manebat,
Cuique esses natus, cuique sodalis, eras.
Heu quam dura preces sprevit, quam surda querelas
Parca, juventutem non miserata tuam!

Many a shower of tears has fallen on your grave—the kind that grief pours forth when combined with tender love. For when you were still alive you were beloved of all, as if you were everyone's son, everyone's friend. Alas, how harsh was the Fate in rejecting those prayers, how deaf in ignoring those lamentations, refusing to pity your youth!

Johnson has shortened the original, mainly by omitting the first couplet, which names the boy as Leontius and says that he died in a foreign land. **6.** The one Fate (*Parca*) does duty for all three, as in Horace, *Odes* 2.16.39.

7.590 Julianus the Egyptian

α. Κλεινὸς Ἰωάννης. β. Θνητός, λέγε. α. Γαμβρὸς ἀνάσσης.
β. Θνητὸς ὅμως. α. Γενεῆς ἄνθος Ἀναστασίου.
β. Θνητοῦ κἀκείνου. α. Βίον ἔνδικος. β. Οὐκέτι τοῦτο
θνητὸν ἔφης· ἀρεταὶ κρείσσονές εἰσι μόρου.

A. Famous was Ioannes. B. Mortal, say. A. The son-in-law of an empress. B. But still, mortal. A. The finest flower of Anastasius's family. B. He, too, was mortal. A. Upright in his life. B. Now *that* attribute you have mentioned is *not* mortal. Virtues are stronger than death.

Clarus Joannes, reginae affinis, ab alto
Sanguine Anastasii; cuncta sepulta jacent:
Et pius, et recti cultor: non illa jacere
Dicam; stat virtus non subigenda neci.

Johannes was famous, a queen's relative, of the lofty blood of Anastasius; all those attributes lie in the grave. He was also pious and a devotee of righteousness. I will not say those attributes lie there; goodness stands fast, not to be conquered by death.

One feels that by going for further compression instead of attempting to reproduce the already compressed dialogue Johnson has sacrificed too much. In the last couplet, however, he has offered a different sort of antithesis in balancing *iacere* with *stat* (4–5).

7.669 Plato

Stella mea, *observas* stellas; Dii me aethera faxint,
Multis ut te oculis sim potis aspicere.

My Stella, you gaze at the stellar scene; would that the gods might make me the sky, that I might be able to look at you with many eyes.

Plato addresses a boy called *Aster* (Star). *Stella* in Latin was also a male's name, but no doubt it would have sounded feminine to Johnson, as it did to Swift. My "stellar scene" for *stellas* is intended merely to indicate the play on words.

1. *observas:* this is a conjecture; the standard text has *observans*. As B points out, in the Greek and in other Latin versions the verb or its equivalent is in the second person singular. This is correct grammar and provides a good antithesis. I doubt if the participle can be justified.

7.676 Anon

Servus Epictetus, mutilato corpore vixi
  Pauperieque Irus, curaque summa Deum.

In life I, Epictetus, was a slave with a crippled body, a very Irus in my poverty, and the greatest favorite of the gods.

The epigram is also printed in O.91, Y.69, B.61, but with *mutilatus* (1) and *prima* for *summa* (2).

1. Epictetus (mid-first to second century AD) was a famous Stoic philosopher. **2.** Irus was the insolent beggar in *Odyssey* 18, who received harsh treatment from the hero. He came to be regarded as the archetypal beggar. **2.** The final "and" causes a surprise; the same effect is in the Greek.

8.137 Gregory Nazianus

Dicite, causidici, gelido nunc marmore magni
  Mugitum tumulus comprimit Amphilochi.

Speak forth, you lawyers; the tomb with its cold marble now suppresses the bellowing of the great Amphilochus.

In the Greek poem Amphilochus is referred to as an orator; for other points cf. 8.120 (wife and children), 121 (brother), 132 (teacher of Gregory), 136 (parents), 138 (sweetness of soul and intellect). But 8.135 notes that he was a lawyer, capable of fiery speech. Johnson took up both points (lawyer, contrast of cold tomb). *Causidicus* ("case-pleader") was used in a derogatory sense by Juvenal (7.106ff., 10.121); this may explain why Johnson uses the contemptuous *mugitum* (expressive of cattle), connected with the Greek μυκάομαι instead of following Gregory, who uses the perfect participle of μύω ("I close" of the lips). In my review of B I was probably wrong to suspect that Johnson had unwittingly confused the two verbs.

9.13 Plato Junior

Ἀνέρα τις λιπόγυιον ὑπὲρ νώτοιο λιπαυγὴς
ἦρε, πόδας χρήσας, ὄμματα χρησάμενος.

A man with defective sight carried on his back a man with defective legs, lending legs, borrowing eyes.

Fert humeris claudum validis per compita caecus,
Hic oculos socio commodat, ille pedes.

A blind man carries on his strong shoulders a lame man over the crossroads; the latter lends his eyes to his companion, the former his legs.

The Greek poet keeps the same man as subject, contriving the complementary effect by changing the active participle "lending" (χρήσας) to the middle participle "borrowing" (χρησάμενος). Johnson characteristically goes for a neat antithesis. "Over the cross-roads" adds a graphic touch, but "strong" is padding.

2. *pes* is sometimes used of the leg rather than the foot.

9.18 Germanicus Caesar

Me, cane vitato, canis excipit alter; eodem
In me animo tellus gignit et unda feras,
Nec mirum; restat lepori conscendere coelum,
Sidereus tamen hic territat, ecce, canis!

After escaping from one dog I was seized by another; land and sea bring forth savage creatures with the same hostility towards me. No wonder. The only recourse for a hare is to rise to the sky; but look! There, too, a starry dog causes panic.

Johnson's version follows the Greek fairly closely; but, as B points out, *nec mirum* should come in v. 1 after the first sentence; it is then explained by *eodem,* etc. The previous epigram (9.17) shows that the second "dog" is a shark or "sea-dog." The third dog is the star Sirius or the constellation Canis Major.

9.29 Antiphilus

Puppe gubernatrix sedisti, Audacia, prima,
  Divitiis acuens aspera corda virum;
Sola rates struis infidas, et dulcis amorem
  Lucri ulciscendum mox nece sola doces.
Aurea secla hominum, quorum spectandus ocellis
  E longinquo itidem pontus et orcus erat.

Audacity, you sat at the helm of the first boat, whetting men's rough hearts with riches. You alone build unreliable vessels, and you alone instil the desire for sweet profits, which must be paid for eventually by death. It was a golden age for men when sea and hell alike had to be viewed with their eyes from afar.

In translating the Greek epigram Johnson apparently had in mind Horace, *Odes* 1.3, which is a reflection on human daring (*audacia*), the quality that led to navigation. Originally Prometheus in his audacity stole fire from heaven. As a result a new lot of fevers descended on the earth, and the doom of death, which was previously remote, now became closer. For the general sentiment see Lovejoy and Boas (1997, index under Navigation).

The Greek poem ends slightly differently: "There was in truth a golden race of mortals, if indeed the sea was viewed from the dry land from afar like Hades." This is mistranslated in the Loeb volume, and the error reappears in B's version of Johnson.

9.39 Musicius

Ad Musas Venus haec: Veneri parete, puellae,
  In vos ne missus spicula tendat Amor.
Haec Musae ad Venerem: Sic Marti, diva, mineris;
  Huc nunquam volitat debilis iste puer.

Venus to the Muses thus: "Obey Venus, girls, or else Cupid may be sent to fire his darts at you." The Muses to Venus thus: "You may threaten Mars like that, o goddess; that feeble boy of yours never flies this way."

9.44 Plato

Hic, aurum ut reperit, laqueum abjicit, alter ut aurum
  Non reperit, nectit quem reperit laqueum.

One man, finding gold, throws away his noose; another, not finding gold, tightens the noose he finds.

The first man, it seems, was carrying a noose or snare for hunting when he discovered gold; the other was looking for gold when he came upon the noose.

9.48 Anon

Antiope satyrum, Danäe aurum, Europa juvencum,
Et cycnum fecit Leda petita Jovem.

When pursued by Jove Antiope made him turn into a satyr, Danae into gold, Europa into a bull, and Leda into a swan.

Johnson's version is the more interesting, for it makes the girls responsible for the god's undignified antics. In the Greek his behavior is due to love.

9.50 Mimnermus

Vive tuo ex animo, vario rumore loquetur
De te plebs audax, hic bene et ille male.

Live according to your heart's desire; the insolent masses will speak of you in various ways—some well, some ill.

Mimnermus has "malicious fellow-citizens"; Johnson expresses a Roman contempt for the mob; cf. Horace, *Odes* 3.1.1 "Odi profanum vulgus et arceo" (I shun the uninitiated mob and ward them off), 2.16.39–40 "malignum / spernere vulgus" (to spurn the malevolent mob).

9.54 Menecrates

Cum procul est, optat, cum venit, quisque senectam
Incusat, semper spe meliora videt.

When old age is far away people wish for it; when it comes they curse it. They always see things in a better light with the aid of hope.

The thought contained in the first two sentences occurs in ancient homilies about discontent; cf. Rudd (1966, 20–21).

The Greek ends ἔστι δ' ἀεὶ κρεῖσσον ὀφειλόμενον (What is due to come is always better); Johnson's *spe* must be an instrumental ablative, even though the following comparative (*meliora*) makes that slightly confusing.

9.55 Lucilius or Menecrates

Optarit quicunque senex sibi longius aevum,
Dignus qui multa in lustra senescat erit.

If any old man wants to live a still longer life, he will deserve to continue ageing for years and years.

2. A *lustrum* was a period of five years. The terrible example of prolonged age was Tithonus.

9.65 Anon

Telluri arboribus ver frondens, sidera coelo,
Graeciae et urbs, urbi est ista propago, decus.

Leafy spring with its trees is an adornment to the earth; the stars to the sky, the city to Greece, and these young folk to the city.

9.66 Antipater of Sidon

Mnemosyne, ut Sappho mellita voce canentem
Audiit, irata est ne nova Musa foret.

When she heard Sappho singing with her honey-sweet voice, Mnemosyne was angry for fear she might turn out to be a new Muse.

The Greek says that amazement seized her (ἕλε θάμβος). Johnson adds a satirical glance at female jealousy.

9.74 Anon

᾿Αγρὸς ᾿Αχαιμενίδου γενόμην ποτέ. νῦν δὲ Μενίππου·
Καὶ πάλιν ἐξ ἑτέρου βήσομαι εἰς ἕτερον.

καὶ γὰρ ἐκεῖνος ἔχειν μέ ποτ' ᾤετο, καὶ πάλιν οὗτος
οἴεται· εἰμὶ δ' ὅλως οὐδενός, ἀλλὰ Τύχης.

I was once Achaemenides's field, now I am Menippus's, and again in the future I shall pass from one man to another. For the former used to think he owned me, and the latter now thinks the same; but actually I belong to no man, but to Chance.

Nunc huic, nunc aliis cedens, cui farra Menippus
Credit, Achaemenidae nuper agellus eram.
Quod nulli proprium versat Fortuna, putabat
Ille suum stolidus, nunc putat ille suum.

Passing now to one man, now to others, I was recently Achaemenides's little field, now Menippus entrusts his corn to me. The former foolishly thought that what belongs to no one and is switched around by Chance was his; now the latter thinks it is his.

Johnson omits the future dimension; he puts the role of Chance in a subordinate clause, thus sacrificing the simplicity of the Greek, and he ends with the foolish delusions of the two men; so again the emphasis is satirical.

Johnson has in mind Horace, *Serm.*2.2.126 (*Fortuna*) and 133–35 (*ager,* two proper names, *nulli proprius, cedet nunc . . . nunc alii*); there is a longer passage on the same theme in *Epist.*2.2.158ff.

9.110 Alpheius

Nunquam jugera messibus onusta, aut
Quos Gyges cumulos habebat auri;
Quod vitae satis est, peto, Macrine:
Mi "nequid nimis" est nimis probatum.

I never desire acres loaded with harvests, or the piles of gold that Gyges had, but what is sufficient for life, Macrinus. To me "Nothing in excess" is exceedingly commendable.

The lines, like the Greek, are hendecasyllables (eleven syllables), a meter used frequently by Catullus.

2. Gyges, king of Lydia (seventh century BC), acquired a vast fortune of gold from the river Pactolus. Like Croesus, he became a symbol of wealth. **3.** Macrinus is unknown. **4.** The Greek says με τέρπει (pleases me); Johnson's *probatum* has a more moral nuance.

9.112 Antipater of Thessalonica

Τρὶς δέκα με πνεύσειν καὶ δὶς τρία μάντιες ἄστρων
  φασίν· ἐμοὶ δ' ἀρκεῖ καὶ δεκὰς ἡ τριτάτη·
τοῦτο γὰρ ἀνθρώποις βιοτῆς ὅρος· ἡ δ' ἐπὶ τούτοις
  Νέστορι· καὶ Νέστωρ δ' ἤλυθεν εἰς ἀΐδην.

The prophets of the stars say I will continue to draw breath for thrice ten and twice three years; and I am content with the third decade. For this is the (right) limit of men's life. Anything more than that is for Nestor; and even Nestor went to Hades.

Vitam a terdecimo sextus mihi finiet annus,
  Astra mathematicos si modo vera docent.
Sufficit hoc votis; flos hic pulcherrimus aevi est,
  Et senium triplex Nestoris urna capit.

The sixth year after the thirtieth will finish my life, if the stars instruct the astrologers aright. That is all I pray for. This is the finest flower of one's lifetime; even the triple old age of Nestor is now contained in an urn.

2. The stars teach the astrologers (possibly wrongly) instead of the astrologers teaching men. **3.** Johnson's line is more colorful. **4.** Johnson's line is more witty. He may have half-remembered Horace (*Odes* 3.1.16) "omne capax movet urna nomen" (The capacious urn shakes every name), and Juvenal's phrase on the mortality of Alexander "sarcophago contentus erit" (*Sat.*10.172).

9.133 Anon

Εἴ τις ἅπαξ γήμας πάλι δεύτερα λέκτρα διώκει,
  ναυηγὸς πλώει δὶς βυθὸν ἀργαλέον.

If a once wedded man again goes in search of another marriage bed, he is a shipwrecked man who sails for a second time on the troublesome deep.

Quisquis adit lectos elata uxore secundos,
  Naufragus iratas ille retentat aquas.

He who, after attending his wife's funeral, enters a second marriage bed, is a shipwrecked sailor who risks again the angry sea.

Johnson sharpens the cynical thought: unlike the Greek poet, he supplies the image of the first wife's funeral and replaces the more general "troublesome" (ἀργαλέον) with the idea of bad temper. He makes some room by including "again" in the verb *retentat.*

9.138 Anon

Me miserum sors omnis habet; florentibus annis
  Pauper eram, nummis diffluit arca senis;
Queis uti poteram quondam Fortuna negavit,
  Queis uti nequeo, nunc mihi praebet opes.

I am unhappy in every phase of life. In the bloom of youth I was poor; my cash box overflows with coins now that I'm old. Earlier, when I could have used the money, Fortune wouldn't let me have it; now when I'm incapable of using it, she makes it available.

Fortune's behavior resembles Johnson's complaint to Lord Chesterfield about patrons.

9.148 Anon

Democrite, invisas homines majore cachinno,
  Plus tibi ridendum secula nostra dabunt.
Heraclite, fluat lacrymarum crebrior imber;
  Vita hominum nunc plus quod misereris habet.
Interea dubito; tecum me causa nec ulla
  Ridere, aut tecum me lacrimare jubet.

Democritus, you would (now) give a louder guffaw on looking at mankind; our age will provide you with more to laugh at. Heraclitus, you would let your tears fall in more copious floods; the life of men has now more for you to pity. Meanwhile I am left in uncertainty; I have no compelling reason to laugh with you, or to weep with you.

Democritus (fifth to fourth century BC) had a major part in the foundation of atomism. He came to be known as "the laughing philosopher," probably on account of his treatise "On Cheerfulness." Heraclitus, who flourished c. 500 BC, stressed that we live in a world of unending change; he was seen as the opposite of Democritus. Johnson has reversed the order of the two sages—perhaps for metrical reasons: *lacrimare* fitted neatly into the end of the final pentameter, whereas *ridere* did not.

1. *majore cachinno* is used of the parasitical Greek in Juvenal 3.100, and *cachinni* occurs in connection with Democritus in Juvenal 10.31. In neither *London* (140 on "the supple Gaul") nor *The Vanity of Human Wishes* (49–68 on Democritus) does Johnson translate the word by the vulgar "guffaw." **5.** *Interea* strictly refers to time; τὸ μεταξύ (between), which the Loeb editor fails to translate, can refer to place, and does so properly here.

9.160 Anon

Exceptae hospitio Musae tribuere libellos
   Herodoto hospitii praemia, quaeque suum.

After being entertained hospitably the Muses gave books to Herodotus as a reward for his hospitality—one each.

The Greek poet orients the reader by beginning with Herodotus; he also varies "entertained" (ὑπεδέξατο) and "hospitality" (φιλοξενίης), whereas Johnson repeats *hospitium.* He must have done so deliberately, though a modern writer would probably have preferred "exceptae laute" (lavishly entertained) or something similar in v. 1.

9.163 Anon

Fert humeris, venerabile onus, Cythereius heros
   Per Troiae flammas densaque tela patrem.
Clamat et Argivis: Vetuli, ne tangite, vita
   Exiguum est Marti, sed mihi grande lucrum.

The Cytherean hero carries his father, a venerable burden, on his shoulders through the flames of Troy and the forest of weapons. He shouts to the Argives, "The life of an old man (keep your hands off him) is a paltry asset to Mars, but a huge one to me."

1. The Cytherean hero is Aeneas—"Cytherean" because his mother, Venus, after her birth came ashore on the island of Cythera off the south coast of the Peloponnese. **2.** His father was Anchises.

9. 250 Honestus

Buccina disjecit Thebarum moenia, struxit
  Quae lyra. Quam sibi non concinit harmonia!

A trumpet threw down the walls of Thebes, which a lyre built up. What an unmusical harmony!

1. The Greek epigram refers to the story that Alexander razed Thebes to the ground to the accompaniment of a flute; cf. 9.253 (Philippus); Gow and Page (1968, 2, 304) give the later sources. As B says, in substituting a trumpet Johnson may have been thinking of *Joshua* 6:20 and the walls of Jericho. **2.** The stones of Thebes are said to have come together at the sound of Amphion's lyre (Apollodorus 3.5.5 with Frazer's note in the Loeb translation)—an allegory for the role of music in producing civic harmony.

9.288 Geminus

Cecropidis gravis hic ponor, Martique dicatus,
  Quo tua signantur gesta, Philippe, lapis.
Spreta jacet Marathon, jacet et Salaminia laurus,
  Omnia dum Macedum gloria et arma premunt.
Sint Demosthenica jurata cadavera voce,
  Stabo illis qui sunt, quique fuere, gravis.

I, a stone, stand here, heavy to the sons of Cecrops and dedicated to Mars, celebrating your achievements, Philip. Marathon lies humbled, and so do the laurels of Salamis—all is crushed by the glorious arms of the Macedonians. Let the voice of Demosthenes swear by the bodies of the dead, I shall weigh heavily on those who are, and those who were once, alive.

1–2. The stone is fictitious. Philip is the Macedonian leader who overthrew the Athenians (the "sons of Cecrops"); he was the father of Alexander. **4.** I have removed the comma after *omnia* which obscures the fact that it is the object of *premunt.* **5.** Demosthenes (*De Corona* 208) declared that the Athenians were right to take the risk of war against Philip, swearing by the Greeks who had fallen in the battles against Persia. I have ignored the transmitted *ut* after *Demosthenica,* which could be defended as introducing a concession, but is not needed and is rightly suspected by editors.

9.304 Parmenio

Qui, mutare vias ausus terraeque marisque,
Trajecit montes nauta, fretumque pedes,
Xerxi, tercentum Spartae Mars obstitit acris
Militibus; terris sit pelagoque pudor!

Xerxes, who dared to change around the pathways of land and sea, crossing the mountains in a boat and the seas on foot, was resisted by Mars in the shape of three hundred warriors from fierce Sparta. Shame on both land and sea!

2. Xerxes dug a canal behind Mt. Athos across the most easterly of the three peninsulas of Chalcidice; he also crossed the Hellespont on a bridge of boats; cf. Juvenal, *Sat.* 10.173–76. **3–4.** The gallant rearguard action of the Spartans at the pass of Thermopylae in 480 BC.

9.359 Posidippus or Plato Comicus

Elige iter vitae, ut possis; rixisque dolisque
Perstrepit omne forum; cura molesta domi est.
Rure labor lassat; mare mille pericula terrent;
Verte solum, fient causa timoris opes;
Paupertas misera est; multae cum coniuge lites
Tecta ineunt; caelebs omnia solus ages;
Proles aucta gravat, rapta orbat, caeca juventae est
Virtus, canities cauta vigore caret.
Ergo optent homines, aut nunquam in luminis oras
Venisse, aut visa luce repente mori.

Choose the course of your life (supposing you could); every city square is loud with the sound of strife and deceit; at home there are tiresome worries. In the country drudgery wears you out; at sea there are a thousand perils to frighten you. Change countries—your money will become a cause of anxiety; poverty is miserable. Many quarrels enter your home along with a wife; as a bachelor you will do everything by yourself. If a child grows up it is a burden; if it dies it leaves you bereft. The manliness of youth is blindly impetuous; cautious grey hair lacks vigour. Therefore men should choose either never to enter the regions of day, or else having seen the light to die on the spot.

2. The forum was where the lawcourts were situated. **3.** The traditional text reads "Rura labor lassat" (Labour wears out the country), which makes no sense. So I have emended to the locative *rure,* which is sufficiently defended by Horace, *Epist.* 1.7.1 "me rure futurum" and 14.10 "rure ego viventem"; Horace in fact never uses the form *ruri.* Earlier support is provided by Plautus, and later by Ovid, *Fasti* 6.671 and *Ars Amatoria* 2.229. The Greek has ἐν δ'ἀγροῖς (In the country). The mistake probably arose from the belief that *mare* was accusative. This raises a more difficult point; for although there is clear support for the ablative form *mare* with a preposition (e.g., Lucretius 1.161, Ovid *Tristia* 5.2.20 and *Ex Ponto* 4.6.46), and perhaps for *mare* without a preposition as an instrumental ablative (Varro Atacinus, "cingitur . . . Libyco mare," frag. 20 (Courtney 1993, 252), it is hard to find an example of *mare* as a locative (Plautus, *Cistellaria* 1.1.14 is not a certain case). Nevertheless, the fact is that Johnson used *mare* to translate . . . ἐν δὲ θαλάσσῃ (on the sea). And even if he found no precedents in later Latin, it is far better to suppose that he was just taking a risk than to accuse him of writing nonsense (a thousand perils terrify the sea). **9.** Having described at length "the vanity of human wishes" Juvenal asks the question: "nil ergo optabunt homines?" (*Sat.* 10.344). "In luminis oras" is a Lucretian expression. **9–10.** The thought, which goes back to Sophocles, *Oedipus at Colonus,* 1224–27, was echoed by Yeats in *A Man Young And Old,* 11 (fourth stanza).

9.360 Metrodorus

Elige iter vitae, ut mavis; prudentia lausque
  Permeat omne forum; vita quieta domi est.
Rus ornat natura; levat maris aspera lucrum;
  Verte solum, donat plena crumena decus;
Pauperies latitat; cum coniuge gaudia multa
  Tecta ineunt, caelebs impediere minus;
Mulcet amor prolis, sopor est sine prole profundus;
  Praecellit juvenis vi, pietate senex.
Nemo optet nunquam venisse in luminis oras,
  Aut periisse; scatet vita benigna bonis.

Choose the course of your life according to your preference. The city squares are all full of wisdom and prestige; life at home is serene. Nature adorns the country; the sea's profits alleviate its roughness. Change countries —a full purse brings esteem; poverty is not visible. With a wife many joys enter your home; as a bachelor you'll have greater freedom. Children's love is charming; without children sleep is deep. Youth excels in strength, old age in piety. Let no one choose either never to enter the regions of day or to die; life is generous, overflowing with blessings.

9.375 Anon

Pectore qui duro, crudos de vite racemos
  Venturi exsecuit, vascula prima meri,
Labraque constrictus semesos, jamque terendos
  Sub pedibus, populo praetereunte, jacit,
Supplicium huic, quoniam crescentia gaudia laesit,
  Det Bacchus, dederat quale, Lycurge, tibi.
Hae poterant uvae laeto convivia cantu
  Mulcere, aut pectus triste levare malis.

The man who with callous heart cuts from the vine the unripe clusters, the first little capsules of the future wine, and then, drawing back his lips, throws them down half chewed to be trampled eventually under the feet of the passing crowd—may Bacchus give him the punishment that he gave you, Lycurgus, for spoiling a pleasure before it has reached full growth. These grapes could have lent charm to a banquet by generating happy song, or relieved a sad heart of its troubles.

6. For attacking Dionysus, Lycurgus was blinded and driven mad; he died after killing his family: see Apollodorus 3.5.1 (Loeb).

9.394 Palladas

Mater adulantum prolesque, Pecunia, curae,
  Teque frui timor est, teque carere dolor.

Money, mother of flatterers and child of anxiety, to possess you is apprehension, and to lack you is misery.

9.444 Eratosthenes Scholasticus

Pulchra est virginitas intacta, at vita periret,
  Omnes si vellent virginitate frui;
Nequitiam fugiens, servata contrahe lege
  Conjugium, ut pro te des hominem patriae.

Immaculate virginity is a fine thing, but life would die out if all women wanted to retain their virginity. Avoid lasciviousness and, keeping the law, enter into marriage, so that you may present your country with a human being to replace yourself.

2. Johnson's dictionary supports this translation of *virginitas;* but the warning given in 3–4 seems to apply at least as much to men—the sort of avuncular advice Johnson would have given Boswell.

9.523 Anon.

Sit tibi, Calliope, Parnassum cura tenenti,
Alter ut adsit Homerus, adest etenim alter Achilles.

Calliope, who inhabit Parnassus, make sure to produce a second Homer, for we already have a second Achilles.

By choosing the idiom "sit tibi cura ut" instead of an imperative and employing *tenenti* instead of a simple genitive, Johnson had to forego any equivalent of the Greek πολύμυθε (literally "of many stories") and μελισσοβότου ("fed on by bees"). I do not know which generals the poets had in mind.

9.530 Anon

Εἰς ἄρχοντα ἀνάξιον

Οὐκ ἐθέλουσα Τύχη σε προήγαγεν, ἀλλ' ἵνα δείξῃ,
ὡς ὅτι καὶ μέχρι σοῦ πάντα ποιεῖν δύναται.

On an Unworthy Official

Not willingly did Fortune promote you, but to show that her universal power reaches even as far as you.

Non Fortuna sibi te gratum tollit in altum;
At docet exemplo, vis sibi quanta, tuo.

It is not because she likes you that Lady Luck is raising you to such a height; no, she is using you as an example to demonstrate how great her power is.

1. According to the Elder Pliny, Lady Luck was "blind, fickle, inconstant, unreliable, and a patroness of the unworthy" (*Nat. Hist.* 2.22). Johnson has improved on the rather vague Greek. **2.** He has added the very Roman idea of an example, but since the crooked man's elevation illustrates the work of Fortuna, it is not a moral example.

9.573 Ammianus

Tu neque dulce putes alienae accumbere mensae.
   Nec probrosa avidae grata sit offa gulae;
Nec ficto fletu, fictis solvare cachinnis,
   Arridens domino collacrymansque tuo,
Laetior haud tecum, tecum neque tristior unquam,
   Sed Miliae ridens atque dolens Miliae.

You ought not to think it agreeable to sit at another man's table. Your greedy gullet should not take pleasure in disreputable gobbets; nor should you dissolve in bogus tears and bogus guffaws, laughing and weeping in concert with your host, not because you are any the happier or any the sadder in yourself, but because you are laughing for Lord Meal and weeping for Lord Meal.

6. The Greek concludes by calling the parasite the embodiment of "fellowship in tears" and "fellowship in laughter": κλαιωμιλίη καὶ γελοωμιλίη. Johnson seems, as B suggests, to be punning on the ending of these words, i.e., *milia.* It is a feeble witticism, but no other explanation seems available.

9.577 Ptolemaeus

Aevi sat novi quam sim brevis; astra tuenti,
   Per certas stabili lege voluta vices,
Tangitur haud pedibus tellus; conviva Deorum
   Expleor ambrosiis exhilarorque cibis.

I know well enough how short-lived a creature I am; but when I gaze at the stars as they revolve through their regular courses in obedience to a fixed law, my feet no longer touch the ground; I am a guest of the gods, feasting and regaling myself on dishes of ambrosia.

1. Johnson has remembered the end of the city mouse's speech to his rustic friend "vive memor quam sis aevi brevis" in Horace, *Serm.*2.6.97.

9.647 Anon

Cum fugere haud possit fractis Victoria pennis,
   Te manet imperii, Roma, perenne decus.

Since Victory with her broken wings cannot fly away, the glory of your empire, Rome, will remain for ever.

2. Strictly *te manet* means "awaits you." I have translated it as if it were *tibi manebit.* Some scholars maintain that "Rome" here is Constantinople; but it is hard to believe that Johnson saw it like that.

9.648 Macedonius

Civis et externus grati; domus hospita nescit
  Quaerere "quis, cujas, quis pater, unde venis?"

Citizen and foreigner are welcome; a hospitable house does not enquire "Who are you, what is your country, who is your father, and where have you just been?"

1. *cujas* (Oxford and Yale) avoids the repetition that *cuius* "Of what family?" (printed in 1787–1825) involves with the following "Who is your father?"

9.654 Julianus Aegyptius

Latrones, alibi locupletum quaerite tecta,
  Assidet huic custos strenua pauperies.

Burglars, look elsewhere for the houses of the rich; a guard is set over this one—stringent poverty.

9.702 Anon

Jupiter hoc templum, ut, siquando relinquit Olympum,
  Atthide non alius desit Olympus, habet.

Jupiter has this temple, so that, whenever he leaves Olympus, in Attica another Olympus should not be lacking.

The epigram refers to the temple of Zeus in Athens, begun in 174 BC but not finished until Hadrian's time (AD 131).

10.26 Lucianus

Hora bonis quasi nunc instet suprema fruaris,
  Plura ut victurus secula, parce bonis:
Divitiis, utrinque cavens, qui tempore parcit,
  Tempore divitiis utitur, ille sapit.

Enjoy your goods as though your last hour were fast approaching; save your goods as though you were going live for ages more. The man who provides for both eventualities, saving his wealth at the right time, using his wealth at the right time—he's the wise one.

Johnson improves on the original by placing the final emphasis on wisdom.

10.27 Lucianus

Impia facta patrans, homines fortasse latebis,
  Non poteris, meditans prava, latere Deos.

If you perpetrate an impious deed, you will perhaps escape the notice of men; you will not succeed, even when contemplating wickedness, in escaping the notice of the gods.

10.28 Lucianus

Omnis vita nimis brevis est felicibus, una
  Nox miseris longi temporis instar habet.

The whole of their lives is too short for the lucky; for the unfortunate one night has the appearance of an age.

10.30 Anon

Gratia ter grata est velox, sin forte moretur
  Gratia vix restat nomine digna suo.

A favor is thrice a favor if it is done promptly; if for some reason it is delayed, the favor remains scarcely any longer worthy of its name.

One is reminded of the proverb “Bis dat qui cito dat” (He gives twice who gives quickly).

10.31 Lucianus

Θνητὰ τὰ τῶν θνητῶν, καὶ πάντα παρέρχεται ἡμᾶς·
ἢν δὲ μή, ἀλλ᾽ ἡμεῖς αὐτὰ παρερχόμεθα.

Mortal are the affairs of mortals, and everything goes past us; or if not, we go past them.

Nil non mortale est mortalibus; omne quod est hi
Praetereunt, aut hos praeterit omne bonum.

Nothing is not mortal to mortals; they go past everything that is, or every blessing goes past them.

For metrical reasons Johnson has moved from the first person to the third.

10.58 Palladas

Terram adii nudus, de terra nudus abibo.
Quid labor efficiet? non nisi nudus ero.

I entered the world with nothing; I shall leave the world with nothing. What will my efforts achieve? I shall still end up with nothing.

It would perhaps be more vivid to translate *nudus* in the first sentence as “naked.” But the rest of the piece implies rather the absence of all possessions, and one has to keep the same expression throughout. Johnson would have had in mind the words from *The Burial of the Dead:* “We brought nothing into this world, and it is certain we can carry nothing out.”

10.60 Palladas

Ditescis, credo, quid restat? quicquid habebis
In tumulum tecum, morte jubente, trahes?

Divitias cumulas, pereuntes neglegis horas,
Incrementa aevi non cumulare potes.

You are growing rich. So I believe. What of the future? Are you going to drag whatever you have into the tomb with you, when death gives the order? You are piling up your riches, unaware that your hours are dwindling. You can't pile up increasing quantities of life.

Johnson has expanded the Greek antithesis "While amassing wealth you are spending time."

10.72 Palladas

Vita omnis scena est ludusque; aut ludere disce
Seria seponens, aut mala dura pati.

Life is all a stage and a play. Either learn to play, setting serious matters aside, or else to endure hard misfortunes.

10.74 Paulus Silentiarius

Prospera sors nec te strepitoso turbine tollat,
Nec menti injiciat sordida cura jugum;
Nam vita incertis incerta impellitur auris,
Omnesque in partes tracta retracta fluit;
Firma manet virtus; virtuti innitere, tutus
Per fluctus vitae sic tibi cursus erit.

Do not allow good fortune to sweep you up in a boisterous whirlwind, or anxious poverty to fasten a yoke on your mind. For life is uncertain, driven by uncertain breezes; and it is pulled to and fro in every direction as it flows along. Integrity stands firm; rely on integrity, and then your voyage will be safe through the waves of life.

1. *Strepitosus* is not to be found in the usual sources. Is it a coinage? **3.** The juxtaposition "incerta incertis" and the chiastic arrangement of noun (a), adjective (b), adjective (a), noun (b) are stylish features impossible in an uninflected language. **4–5.** Life as a voyage is, of course, an age-old idea. See, for example, Horace, *Odes*

2.10.1–4 with Nisbet and Hubbard's Greek and Latin parallels (1978), the last two stanzas of *Odes* 3.29, and *Epistles* 2.2.201–2 with Brink's notes (1982).

10.84 Palladas

Natus eram lacrymans, lacrymans e luce recedo;
   Sunt quibus a lacrymis vix vacat ulla dies.
Tale hominum genus est, infirmum, triste, misellum,
   Quod mors in cineres solvit, et abdit humo.

I was born crying; crying I withdraw from life. There are people for whom scarcely a day is free from tears. Such is the race of men—weak, sad, wretched, a thing that death reduces to ashes and hides in the ground.

2. Johnson is superior to his model, which says ("I found the whole of life in the midst of many tears"). **4.** Johnson also strengthens the Greek by bringing in the agency of death.

10.93 Palladas

Fortunae malim adversae tolerare procellas,
   Quam domini ingentis ferre supercilium.

I would rather endure the storms of adverse fortune than put up with the superciliousness of a great lord.

Johnson makes the epigram personal; by the "great lord" no doubt he means people like Lord Chesterfield, who failed to help him when he needed support.

10.98 Palladas

Cum tacet indoctus, sapientior esse videtur,
   Et morbus tegitur, dum premit ora pudor.

When an uneducated man keeps quiet, he seems to be wiser than he is, and his ailment is concealed as long as diffidence seals his lips.

2. The Greek says τὸν λόγον ἐγκρύπτων, ὡς πάθος αἰσχρότατον (Hiding his speech like a disgraceful disease). This is more precise; Johnson does not mention speech directly, and this, along with his word order, gives the impression that the lack of education in general is the ailment in question.

10.108 Anon

Seu prece poscatur, seu non, da Jupiter omne
Magne bonum, omne malum et poscentibus abnue nobis.

Mighty Jove, grant us every blessing whether we ask for it or not; refuse every evil even when we do ask for it.

The address to Jupiter and the choice of satirical hexameters give this a pagan feel. More specifically, the idea that we often pray for things that will hurt us recalls Juvenal 10.8–9 "nocitura toga, nocitura petuntur / militia" (Things that will prove disastrous are requested in peace, things that will prove disastrous [are requested] in war). At the beginning of the satire these misguided prayers are often answered, e.g., "evertere domos totas optantibus ipsis / di faciles" (The gods often obligingly wreck entire households at the request of the occupants); in *The Vanity of Human Wishes* 14–15 Johnson attributes these malign acts to Vengeance and Fate—but not, of course, to God. At the end of the satire, however, Juvenal says that the gods will decide what is best for us (347ff.)—an idea that Johnson could render in Christian terms.

10.113 Anon

Non opto, aut precibus posco ditescere, paucis
Sit contenta mihi vita, dolore carens.

I do not wish, nor do I ask in prayer, to become rich; I should like my life to be contented with a little—but free from sorrow.

10.119 Anon

Recta ad pauperiem tendit, cui corpora cordi est
Multa alere, et multas aedificare domos.

He is making straight for poverty, the man who enjoys feeding many bodies and building many houses.

The Greek poet put Johnson's opening sentence at the end, where it produces an effective surprise.

10.123 Aesopus

Quae sine morte fuga est vitae, quam turba malorum
   Non vitanda gravem, non toleranda facit?
Dulcia dat natura quidem, mare, sidera, terras,
   Lunaque quas et sol itque reditque vias.
Terror inest aliis moerorque, et siquid habebis
   Forte boni, ultrices experiere vices.

What escape other than death is there from a life made burdensome by a host of ills which cannot be avoided or endured? Nature, to be sure, gives sweet delights—sea, stars, countries, and the paths which sun and moon travel again and again. Terror and grief are present in other things, and if you happen to have any good luck, you will pay for it when it is duly reversed.

10.124 Glyco

Quandoquidem passim nulla ratione feruntur
   Cuncta, cinis cuncta et ludicra, cuncta nihil.

As all things everywhere are borne along in a senseless fashion, all is ashes and absurdity; all is nothing.

Johnson has given sharper point to the epigram by putting the first sentence of the Greek at the end.

11.50 Automedon

Faelix ante alios nullius debitor aeris;
   Hunc sequitur caelebs; tertius, orbe, venis.

Nec male res cessit, subito si funere sponsam,
  Ditatus magna dote, recondis humo.
His sapiens lectis, Epicurum quaerere frustra
  Quales sint monades, qua *sit* inane, sinas.

Happy above all others is the man who has no debts; next comes the bachelor; and you, childless one, come third. Nor have things turned out badly if your bride dies suddenly and you bury her, enriched by a large dowry. Once you have acquired wisdom by reading these truths, you may leave Epicurus to conduct his futile enquiry into the nature of atoms and the whereabouts of void.

6. The traditional text has *fit,* which, as W. S.Watt pointed out to me, is a misreading of a long s. A subjunctive is required parallel to *sint.*

11.53 Anon

Vita rosae brevis est; properans si carpere nolis,
  Quaerenti obveniet mox sine flore rubus.

The life of a rose is brief. If you refuse to be quick and pluck it, you will soon, when you look for it, be confronted by a thorn without a bloom.

11.118 Callicter

Haud lavit Phido, haud tetigit; mihi febre calenti
  In mentem ut venit nominis interii.

Dr. Enema did not irrigate me or lay a hand on me; when I was burning with a fever, I thought of his name, and gave up the ghost.

"Phido" in Greek was a proper name. Unfortunately the pun is not available in English.

11.145 Anon

En Sexto, Sexti meditatur imago, silente;
Orator statua est, statuaeque orator imago.

Look, whereas Sextus is silent, Sextus's statue is rehearsing his speech. The statue is the orator; the orator is merely the image of his statue.

In this triumph of art the statue is more lifelike than the original. As Johnson has changed the Greek portrait to a Roman statue, one wonders if, in rendering the Greek μελετᾷ by its Latin equivalent (*meditatur*), he half-remembered Juvenal 7.124–28, where the equestrian statue of a second-rate lawyer is amusingly confused with the man himself (*ipse*), and the man is said to be rehearsing battle in his one-eyed statue (statua meditatur proelia lusca). We know that Johnson had all the satires by heart (Hill and Powell 1934, 1:192–93).

11.167 Pollianus

Cur opulentus eges? tua cuncta in foenore ponis.
  Sic aliis dives, tu tibi pauper agis.

Why is a rich man like you in distress? You put out all you have in loans. So while to others you are rich, you act like a pauper to yourself.

11.176 Lucilius

Hermem Deorum nuncium, pennis levem,
Quo rege gaudent Arcades, furem boum,
Hujus palaestrae qui vigil custos stetit,
Clam nocte tollit Aulus, et ridens ait:
Praestat magistro saepe discipulus suo.

Hermes, the messenger of the gods, who can fly on wings, the king in whom the Arcadians rejoice, the thief of oxen, who stood alert as guard over this gymnasium, was secretly carried off at night by Aulus, who said with a smile: "The pupil often surpasses his teacher."

The Greek epigram is in iambic trimeters, which Johnson follows.

11.186 Nicarchus

Nycticorax cantat lethale, sed ipsa canenti
Demophilo auscultans nycticorax moritur.

The night-raven's song causes death, but on hearing Demophilus sing the night-raven herself dies.

11.213 Leonidas

Menodotum pinxit Diodorus, et exit imago,
Praeter Menodotum, nullius absimilis.

Diodorus painted Menodotus, and the portrait turned out to resemble everyone *except* Menodotus.

At the beginning of the *Ars Poetica* Horace talks about incompetent painters (19–21); then he goes on to incompetent potters: "amphora coepit / institui: currente rota cur urceus exit?" (21–22) (The job began as a wine-jar; why, as the wheel revolves, does it turn out to be a jug?).

11.391 Lucilius

Murem Asclepiades sub tecto ut vidit avarus,
Quid tibi, mus, mecum, dixit, amice, *domi?*
Mus blandum ridens, respondit, pelle timorem;
Hic, bone vir, sedem, non alimenta, peto.

When he saw a mouse under his roof, the miser Asclepiades said: "What do you want with me, dear mouse, in my home?" With a charming smile the mouse replied: "Never fear, good sir; here I am looking for accommodation, not food."

2. In the traditional text the line ends with another *tibi,* which is impossible. In correspondence Watt convincingly restored *domi* on the basis of the Greek pentameter: καὶ "τί ποιεῖς," φησίν, "φίλτατε μῦ παρ' ἐμοί;" (And what, my dear mouse, he said, are you doing at my place?).

11.430 Lucianus

Qui pascit barbam si crescit mente, Platoni,
  Hirce, parem nitido te tua barba facit.

If a man grows in wisdom by growing a beard, your beard, Mr Goat, makes you the equal of the brilliant Plato.

2. I can find no classical authority for *nitidus* used either of fame or intellect; but that has to be Johnson's point.

11.432 Lucianus

Pulicibus morsus, restincta lampade, stultus
  Exclamat: Nunc me cernere desinitis!

When bitten by fleas, a fool put out the light crying, "Now you can"t see me any more!'

1. "lampade stultus" is just one of many examples which show that Johnson found nothing objectionable in keeping a syllable short when a short vowel is followed by two consonants, the first of which is s. See the note on "unda Scamandri" (Catullus 64.357) in Fordyce (1961).

13.3 Theocritus

Poeta, lector, hic quiescit Hipponax,
Si sis scelestus, praeteri procul marmor:
At te bonum si noris, et bonis natum,
Tutum hic sedile, et si placet, sopor tutus.

The poet Hipponax, reader, lies here at rest. If you happen to be a rogue, give the marble a wide berth. But if you know you're a good man of good family, here is a safe spot to sit down, and, if you wish, a safe spot for a nap.

The meter, as with the original, is the so-called "limping iambic" ("choliambic" or "scazon"), i.e., an iambic trimeter, like 11.176 above, but with the penultimate syllable long. Theocritus chose this meter because it was supposed to have been invented by Hipponax himself, a sixth-century poet famous for his invective.

16 (Appendix Planudea).1 Damacetus

Non Argos pugilem, non me Messana creavit;
Patria Sparta mihi est, patria clara virum.
Arte valent isti, mihi robore *vincere* solo est,
Convenit ut natis, inclyta Sparta, tuis.

It was not Argos, no, nor Messana that made me a boxer; my country is Sparta, a country famed for its men. Those other fellows prevail through art; my gift is to win by sheer strength, as is appropriate, illustrious Sparta, for your sons.

3. The traditional text has *vivere* (to live); but the poet is not talking about life-styles, but about skills in the ring. The Greek has βίᾳ κρατέω (I conquer by strength), which balances τεχνάεντες as *robore* balances *arte.* Johnson has changed the Greek wrestling to boxing, which is perhaps slightly less appropriate to sheer strength.

16.16 Anon

Quod nimium est fit ineptum; hinc, ut dixere priores,
Et melli nimio fellis amaror inest.

What is too much becomes out of place; hence, as our forefathers said, even too much honey has the bitterness of gall.

16.87 Julianus Aegyptius

Arti ignis lucem tribui, tamen artis et ignis
Nunc ope supplicii vivit imago mei.
Gratia nulla hominum mentes tenet, ista Promethei
Munera muneribus si retulere fabri

I brought to art the light of fire; yet now with the aid of art and fire the image of my punishment lives on. Gratitude has no hold on the minds of men, if that is what the metalworkers have given in return for Prometheus's gift.

1. Johnson's Latin is so condensed that it is barely intelligible without the Greek, which itself is not easy: Τέχνης πυρσὸν ὄπασσα φερέσβιον (I brought [to mortals] the life-giving fire of art). Prometheus stole fire from the gods, which made possible the casting of lifelike metal statues. **1–2.** The reference is to a statue showing his punishment, which was to have his liver eternally torn by a vulture.

16.168 Anon
On the Cnidian Aphrodite

Γυμνὴν εἶδε Πάρις με, καὶ Ἀγχίσης, καὶ Ἄδωνις·
τοὺς τρεῖς οἶδα μόνους· Πραξιτέλης δὲ πόθεν;

Unde *hoc* Praxiteles? nudam vidistis Adoni,
Et Pari, et Anchisa, non alius, Venerem.

How did Praxiteles manage this? You, Adonis, Paris, and Anchises, have seen Venus naked, but nobody else has.

The Greek is probably spoken by the Cnidian Aphrodite herself; and the second line ends "But how did Praxiteles come to do so?" Unfortunately *unde,* being metrically different from πόθεν, could not be used to end the Latin pentameter; so Johnson transferred the question to the beginning. But the traditional reading "Unde hic Praxiteles?" is awkward; for without anything coming before it the question would naturally mean "Where does this Praxiteles come from?" The rest of the epigram has to be read before the question can be understood. The masculine nominative *hic* cannot refer either to this statue or this situation. The neuter accusative *hoc,* however, can refer to the *opus;* which *opus* is meant then becomes clear—it is Venus's statue. On balance, then, it seemed justifiable to alter one letter of the text.

16.209 Anon

Sufflato accendis quisquis carbone lucernam,
Corde meo accendas; ardeo totus ego.

You, whoever you are, who light your lamp by blowing on a piece of charcoal, light it from my heart; I am all ablaze.

This very old conceit goes back to pieces by Valerius Aedituus and Porcius Licinus (probably late second century BC). The former reads:

Quid faculam praefers, Phileros, qua est nil opus nobis?
ibimus sic, lucet pectore flamma satis.
istanc <aut> potis est vis saeva extinguere venti
aut imber caelo concitus praecipitans;
at contra hunc ignem Veneris, nisi si Venus ipsa,
nullast quae possit vis alia opprimere.

Why do you hold your torch out in front, Phileros? I have no need of it. I'll go like this [i.e., torchless]; the flame from my heart is bright enough. Your flame can be extinguished by the wild force of the wind or by the swift rain-shower hurtling down from the sky; but this flame of Venus on the other hand cannot be quenched by any other power than Venus herself.

The latter reads:

Custodes ovium teneraeque propaginis, agnum,
quaeritis ignem? ite huc, <totus hic> ignis homost.
si digito attigero, incendam silvam simul omnem,
omne pecus; flammast omnia quae video.

Guardians of the flocks and their young offspring, the lambs, are you looking for fire? Come this way; this man is all fire. If I touch it with my finger I shall thereby set alight the whole wood, the whole flock; everywhere I look is ablaze.

See Aulus Gellius, *Noctes Atticae,* 19.9.12–13 (Loeb ed. vol. 3), Courtney (1993, 70, 73 and 82); cf. also *The Greek Anthology* 9.15 and 12.79.

16.326 Anon

Dat tibi Pythagoram pictor; quod ni ipse tacere
Pythagoras mallet, vocem habuisset opus.

The painter presents you with Pythagoras; had Pythagoras not chosen to remain silent, the picture would have had a voice.

1–2. In addition to his scientific researches into mathematics, music, and astronomy, Pythagoras's teaching had a quasi-mystical element, which was reflected in the master's brotherhood, with its initiations, secret doctrines, and passwords. Diogenes Laertius (8.10) conveys the tradition that for five years his students had to keep silent; then, after passing an examination, they were admitted to his house. The tradition of Pythagoras's secretiveness is referred to by Isocrates, Porphyry, Iamblichus, and Plutarch. See Guthrie (1962, 1:149–52).

16.331 Agathias

Clara Cheroneae soboles, Plutarche, dicavit
  Hanc statuam ingenio Roma benigna tuo.
Das bene collatos, quos Roma et Graecia jactat,
  Ad Divos paribus passibus ire duces;
Sed similem, Plutarche, tuae describere vitam
  Non poteras, regio non tulit ulla parem.

Plutarch, famous son of Chaeronea, an appreciative Rome has set up this statue to your genius. You well compare the leaders who are the pride of Rome and Greece, enabling them to proceed with parallel steps to the gods. But you could not recount any life similar to your own, Plutarch; for no region has produced a parallel.

1. I do not know on what authority Johnson shortened the *ae* of Chaeronea (αι in Greek). Plutarch was born before AD 50 and died after 120. His *Parallel Lives* has been a major influence on western literature.

16.364 Leontius

Mente senes olim juvenis, Faustine, premebas,
  Nunc juvenum terres robore corda senex.

Once, Faustinus, when young, you would overawe the old by your mind; now that you're old, you alarm the hearts of the young by your strength.

The second couplet of the Greek runs:

δεύτερα δ'εὕρετο πάντα τεὸς πόνος, ὅς σε γεραίρει
  πρέσβυν ἐν ἠιθέοις, ἐν δὲ γέρουσι νέον.

But your efforts, which won you honor as an old man among the young and as a young man among the old, found everything inferior.

This rather cryptic couplet seems to mean "Your achievements have proved you superior to young and old alike."

Johnson has:

> Laevum at utrumque decus, juveni quod praebuit olim
> Turba senum, juvenes nunc tribuere seni.

But each honor—that which the crowd of old men awarded you formerly as a youth, and that which the young men now give you as an old man—is a left-handed compliment.

The difficulty is that the series of epigrams by Leontius from 357–78 are all complimentary, including nos. 358.1–2, 359.3–4, and 372.3–6, which are very close to this in form.; cf. also Thomas's epigram on Faustinus, no. 383. Rather than assuming that Johnson has misunderstood the piece, one ought perhaps to conclude that he has deliberately given it a satirical twist.

O.259, Y.340, B.260

Simonides (?)
Thucydides, 6.59

The first couplet of the Greek runs:

> ἀνδρὸς ἀριστεύσαντος ἐν Ἑλλάδι τῶν ἐφ' ἑαυτοῦ
> Ἱππίου Ἀρχεδίκην ἥδε κέκευθε κόνις

This dust covers Archedice, daughter of Hippias, the most distinguished man in the Greece of his day.

The first line of the Latin text is a mess:

> Prolem Hippi, et sua qua meliorem secula nullum
> Videre, Archidicen haec tumulavit humus;

Hippi is a strange way of rendering the Greek genitive *Hippiou* (where the *-ou* is shortened in hiatus). Watt proposes to read *Hippiae* (scanned as a disyllable *"Hippyae"*) for *Hippi et.* This produces a regular genitive form of the Greek name in Latin; cf. *Leonidae* from the Greek *Leonidas;* it also gets rid of the problematic *et.* If *et* is retained, the *qua*-clause refers to Archidice, which falsifies the Greek; also *nullum* has then to be changed to *nullam,* and the problem about the form of *Hippi* remains. Finally, as B noticed, if the relative clause refers to Hippias, as it should, *qua* has to be changed to *quo.* The whole epigram will then read:

Prolem *Hippiae,* sua *quo* meliorem secula nullum
  Videre, Archidicen haec tumulavit humus;
Quam, regum sobolem, nuptam, matrem atque sororem
  Fecerunt nulli sors titulique gravem.

Archedice, the daughter of Hippias, who was as fine a man as his age ever saw, is buried in this grave. Though she was the child, wife, mother, and sister of kings, her station and titles did not make her overbearing to anyone.

For the background to the Greek epigram see Campbell (1967, 396–97) and Page (1981, 239–40).

O.259, Y.340, B.260

Cleanthes
Epictetus, *Encheiridion, 53.1*

Me, Rex Deorum, tuque, duc, Necessitas,
Quo lege vestra vita me feret mea.
Sequar libenter; sin reluctari velim,
Fiam scelestus, nec tamen minus sequar.

O king of the gods, and you, necessity, lead me wherever my life shall take me according to your law. I shall follow gladly; if I should wish to resist, I should thereby be a transgressor, but I should follow you nonetheless.

Cleanthes (331–232 BC), who succeeded Zeno as head of the Stoa, stressed the religious element in the system. These lines, addressed to Zeus and Destiny, are quoted by Epictetus (mid-first to mid-second century AD) at the end of his *Encheiridion* (53). Johnson follows the Greek quite closely. In his looser version Seneca (*Moral Epistles* 107.11) added a much-quoted fifth line, which summed up the point: "ducunt volentem fata, nolentem trahunt" (the fates lead the one who is willing, drag the one who is not).

O.259, Y.340, B.261

Unidentified

Cogitat aut loquitur nil vir, nil cogitat uxor;
  Felici thalamo non, puto, rixa strepit.

The husband neither thinks nor says anything, the wife does not think anything; in that happy boudoir, I fancy, there are no noisy quarrels.

For a discussion of the piece's provenance see B.261–62.

O.260, Y.341, B.147

Septem Aetates

Prima parit terras aetas; siccatque secunda;
Evocat Abramum dein tertia; quarta relinquit
Aegyptum; templo Solomonis quinta superbit;
Cyrum sexta timet; laetatur septima Christo.

The Seven Ages

The first age gives birth to the world; the second dries it out; the third then calls forth Abraham; the fourth leaves Egypt; the fifth glories in the temple of Solomon; the sixth lives in fear of Cyrus; the seventh rejoices in Christ.

For the cultural background see B.148 and his references. **1.** Dries it out after the flood. **4.** Cyrus the Great, founder of the Persian empire; died 530 BC.

O.260, Y.342, B.148

A Meditation

Luce collustret mihi pectus alma,
Pellat et tristes animi tenebras,
Nec sinat semper tremere ac dolere
    Gratia Christi;

Me Pater tandem reducem benigno
Summus amplexu foveat, beato
Me gregi Sanctus socium beatum
    Spiritus addat.

May the grace of Christ brighten my heart with kindly light, banish the gloomy darkness of my mind, and prevent me from living in constant dread and misery. May the Almighty Father bring me back at the last and comfort me in his loving arms; may the Holy Spirit add me to the blessed flock as a blessed member.

The stanzas are in the Sapphic meter.

O.261, Y.342, B.157

In Rivum a Mola Stoana Lichfeldiae diffluentem

Errat adhuc vitreus per prata virentia rivus,
  Quo toties lavi membra tenella puer;
Hic delusa rudi frustrabar brachia motu,
  Dum docuit blanda voce natare pater.
Fecerunt rami latebras, tenebrisque diurnis
  Pendula secretas abdidit arbor aquas.
Nunc veteres duris periere securibus umbrae,
  Longinquisque oculis nuda lavacra patent.
Lympha tamen cursus agit indefessa perennis,
  Tectaque qua fluxit, nunc et aperta fluit.
Quid ferat externi velox, quid deterat aetas,
  Tu quoque securus res age, Nise, tuas.

On the Stream at Stowe Mill, Lichfield

The river, still glassy, flows through the green meadows in which as a boy I so often bathed my young limbs. Here I would vainly thrash my arms, which got nowhere with their inexpert movements, while my father with his calm voice taught me to swim. The branches made a hiding place, and an overhanging tree covered the hidden waters in darkness even by day. Now the shadows of old have fallen victim to cruel axes; and the bathing place lies exposed to distant eyes. The water, however, unwearyingly continues on its course from year to year, and where it once flowed unseen it now still flows, though in the open. You too, Nisus, continue your daily course, indifferent to what swift time may bring in from the world outside, and what it may wear away.

4. It seems that Johnson grew up to be quite a strong swimmer (Hill and Powell 1934, 2.299). **12.** Nisus is usually identified with Edmund Hector, but B puts forward a case for Bennet Langton. Nisus and his younger friend, Euryalus, figure memorably in *Aeneid* 5.286–361 and 9.176–449. In military terms they are a pair of dangerous hotheads, but as they are young, handsome, and doomed, Virgil treats them with notable sensitivity and indulgence. The associations of tenderness and nostalgia chime well with the mood of the poem; for it is clear that, however fleetingly, Johnson pictures his boyhood self as Euryalus. It is pushing the parallel too far, however, to suggest that the recipient is being assured that Johnson will die before him; for in *Aeneid* 9.443–45 Nisus dies only seconds after Euryalus.

O.262, Y.349, B.149

Jactura Temporis

Hora perit furtim laetis, mens temporis aegra
Pigritiam incusat, nec minus hora perit.

Waste of Time

The hour passes away unnoticed by the happy; the suffering mind rails against time's sluggishness, but the hour passes away just the same.

Loading a Ship

Quas navis recipit, quantum sit pondus aquarum,
Dimidium tanti ponderis intret onus.

Work out the weight of water that a ship holds; then let a load of half that weight be taken on board.

The Speed of Sound

Quot vox missa pedes abit horae parte secunda?
  Undecies centum denos quater adde duosque.

How many feet does the voice when emitted cover in the second division of an hour? Eleven times one hundred, four tens, plus two.

This was the standard figure throughout the eighteenth century.

I have followed Y and B in giving the last two of the above epigrams separate headings. **1.** The phrase "vox missa" may have occurred to Johnson because of Horace's famous aphorism (*Ars Poetica* 390) "nescit vox missa reverti" (Once it has been sent forth the spoken word cannot find its way back). Seconds are the second division, just as minutes are the first.

O.263–64, Y.350–51, B.152–53

Geographia Metrica

His Tempelmanni numeris descripseris orbem.
Cum sex centuriis Judaeo millia septem.
Myrias Aegypto cessit bis septima pingui.
Myrias adsciscit sibi nonagesima septem
Imperium qua Turca ferox exercet iniquum.
  Undecies binas decadas et millia septem
Sortitur Pelopis tellus quae nomine gaudet.
  Myriadas decies septem numerare jubebit
Pastor Arabs: decies octo sibi Persa requirit.
  Myriades sibi pulcra duas, duo millia poscit
Parthenope. Novies vult tellus mille Sicana.
Papa suo regit imperio ter millia quinque.
Cum sex centuriis numerat sex millia Tuscus.
Centuria Ligures augent duo millia quarta.
Centuriae octavam decadem addit Lucca secundae.
  Ut dicas, spatiis quam latis imperet orbi
Russia, myriadas ter denas adde trecentis:
Sardiniam cum sexcentis sex millia complent.
  Cum sexagenis, dum plura recluserit aetas,

Myriadas ter mille homini dat terra colendas.
Vult sibi vicenas millesima myrias addi,
Vicenis quinas, Asiam metata celebrem.
Se quinquagenis octingentesima jungit
Myrias, ut menti pateat tota Africa doctae.
Myriadas septem decies Europa ducentis
Et quadragenis quoque ter tria millia jungit.
Myriadas denas dat, quinque et millia, sexque
Centurias, et tres decadas Europa Britannis.
Ter tria myriadi conjungit millia quartae,
Centuriae quartae decades quinque Anglia nectit.
Millia myriadi septem foecunda secundae
Et quadragenis decades quinque addit Ierne,
Quingentis quadragenis socialis adauget
Millia Belga novem.
Ter sex centurias Hollandia jactat opima.
Undecimum Camber vult septem millibus addi.

A Measurement of the Globe

You could make a survey of the globe using these figures from Templeman: seven thousand plus six hundred square miles for Palestine, twice seven times ten thousand have fallen to fertile Egypt. Where he holds sway over his wicked empire, the fierce Turk has appropriated ninety-seven times ten thousand. The land rejoicing in the name of Pelops has as its share seven thousand plus two hundred and twenty.The Arab shepherd will bid you count seventy times ten thousand. The Persian demands for himself eighty times ten thousand. Lovely Parthenope calls for twenty thousand plus two thousand. The land of Sicily wants nine times a thousand. The pope rules three times five thousand in his kingdom. The Tuscan counts six thousand plus six hundred. The Ligurians increase two thousand by four hundred. Lucca adds eighty to two hundred. To work out the breadth of the regions over which Russia rules, add three hundred thousand to thirty times a hundred thousand. Six thousand plus six hundred make up the size of Sardinia. Until time reveals more, the earth grants three thousand times ten thousand plus sixty times ten thousand for the habitation of mankind. To measure populous Asia, ten million, two hundred thousand, and fifty thousand are required. Five hundred thousand is added to eight million so that the whole of Africa may lie open to the scholar's mind. Europe adds seven hundred thousand to two million, and nine thousand to forty thousand. To the Britons Europe assigns one hundred thousand plus five thousand plus six hundred and thirty. England joins nine thousand to forty thousand and then adds four hundred and fifty. Fertile Ireland adds seven thousand to twenty thousand, and fifty to four hundred. Our ally the Belgian increases nine thousand by five hundred and forty. Rich Holland boasts eighteen hundred. The Welshman wants seven thousand plus eleven.

1. Thomas Templeman's *A New Survey of the Globe* was published in 1729. **11.** Parthenope is Naples. **12.** *Papa* is late Latin, related to the Greek πάππας (father). **14.** Johnson is thinking particularly of Genoa. **34.** Johnson would hardly have intended the line to be incomplete, for he was strongly against the idea that Virgil meant to leave his half lines unfinished.

O.266, Y.351–2, B.163

Prayer

Summe Deus, cui caeca patent penetralia cordis;
  Quem nulla anxietas, nulla cupido fugit;
Quem nil vafrities peccantum subdola celat;
  Omnia qui spectans, omnia ubique regis;
Mentibus afflatu terrenas ejice sordes
  Divino, sanctus regnet ut intus amor:
Eloquiumque potens linguis torpentibus affer,
  Ut tibi laus omni semper ab ore sonet:
Sanguine quo gentes, quo secula cuncta piavit,
  Haec nobis Christus promeruisse velit!

Almighty God, to whom the dark recesses of our hearts are open, whom no worry, no desire escapes, from whom sinners in their sly deceit conceal nothing, who seeing all things, rulest all things everywhere; by thy divine inspiration cast out the earthly filth from our minds, so that holy love may reign within. Bring a powerful eloquence to our deadened tongues, so that thy praises may sound for ever from all men's lips. Through the blood by which he atoned for all peoples and all ages may Christ consent to earn these blessings on our behalf.

To show how Johnson has expanded his source so as to meet the requirements of meter, the *Collect for the Communion Service* is printed here: "Almighty God, unto whom all hearts be open, all desires known, and from whom no secrets are hid; Cleanse the thoughts of our hearts by the inspiration of thy Holy Spirit, that we may perfectly love thee, and worthily magnify thy holy Name, through Christ our Lord. Amen."

Johnson's prayer is dated December 5, 1784. This, as far as we know, was his last Latin poem. His final English prayer, printed by B, was written on the same day. Eight days later he died.

4

Contributions to Poems by Others

O.429–31, B.164–66 Revision of Geoffrey Walmsley's Latin translation of John Byrom's "Colin and Phebe." Johnson's distichs (J) are followed by Stephen Barrett's responses (B), who takes on the persona of Virgil's Corydon.

J: Traduxi, Aonides, placidas quam leniter horas,
  Dum mihi *Phoebe* aderat blandula, grata comes!
B: Pectore (vix dicam) quot, quantaque gaudia sensi!
  Quis mage quam *Corydon* sorte beatus erat?
J: Eheu! hinc abiit numquam reditura puella,
  Atratis facies jam nova rebus adest.
B: Cur veris perit omnis honos? Cur gloria ruris?
  En! teneo! - Has veneres, hoc decus illa dedit.
J: Pascere oves, lusuque simul cum virgine tempus
  Fallere, vel somnos cespite inire leves,
B: Quam mihi jucundum! praesens dum nympha juvabat,
  Laetitia insanus quo rapiebar amans!
J: Nunc tamen, infelix!—quantum, heu! mutatus ab illo!
  Fervida quam tacita viscera bile tument!
B: Nympha abiit, fugitque simul mea sola voluptas;
  Cor! grave cor! luctus pondera ferre nequit.
J: Qui liquido lapsu tremulus fluitare solebat
  Rivulus, et placidis saxa lavare sonis,
B: Scis puer Idalie! arrisit modo nympha, placebat
  Curriculo hisce oculis, auribus hisce sono.
J: *Hac* absente tamen, ripae dum margine oberro,
  Increpo sic surdis jam truculentus aquis;
B: "Quid salis unda jocosa? quid haec mihi murmura volvis?
  Desine; neu lacrymis obstrepe, lympha, meis!"
J: Dum tenerae circum saltarent matribus agnae,
  Dum mecum indoctos risit & illa choros,

B: "Ludite vos, alacres!—Saturnia tempora!" dixi;
Alma viget veris jam Cytherea comes.
J: Nunc dum praetereunt—'fugite hinc! pecus ite molestum!
Ite"—& gramineo vellera fasce peto.
B: Sistite! lascivae, facit haec lascivia tristem;
Cura haud tristitiae vos tenet ulla meae.
J: Quam mihi fidus *Hylax* placuit, dum saepe moveret
Caudam, & blandiloquis solveret ora sonis!
B: Huc ades, O chare, inquit, amicule, laeta, manuque
Permulsit nivea molliter illa caput.
J: Nunc, dum blanditur, petulantia verba rependo,
Et properat duri verbera ferre pedi.
B: Verbera plura manent,—nec *Hylax,* absente puella,
Gaudeat, at mecum triste gemente, gemat.
J: Qualia, Dii! vidi, dum me mea nympha secuta est!
Floribus et campis gratia quanta fuit!
B: Hinc virgulta juvant, et opacae frondibus umbrae;
Hinc rident segetes—et nemus inde viret.
J: Jam formosa abiit, jamque haec decus omne reliquit,
Nec mihi jam, quondam quae nituere, nitent.
B: Fallax nympha diu magicis me lusit ocellis:
Vana mihi mentem cepit imago diu.
J: Indocili nobis resonabant carmine sylvae,
Dat philomela, simul turdus, alauda, modos.
B: Aura susurrabat zephyri, balantibus agnis,
Dum strepit ad nostros laeta cicada pedes.
J: Abscessit—volucrum, mira dulcedine, sensus
Quae tetigere prius carmina, moesta gravant.
B: Vox erat (experto jam credite) mellea nymphae,
Quae liquidum, ante alias, carmen ad astra tulit.
J: Quid, rosa, mutatis *foliis* nunc arida palles;
Purpureum violae quid posuere decus?
B: Quid nec habent solitos languentia germina odores?
Nec pratis idem est, qui fuit ante color?
J: Aemula! fulsistis varios induta nitores,
Pulchrum ut ferret onus pulchrior illa sinu.
B: Dulce fuit vobis nostrae placuisse puellae,
Nec non marmoreo pectore dulce mori.
J: Quam lente incedit tempus! jam nympha redito;
Uror qua Zephyri frigora blanda meant.
B: Quo quaeram, ut gravidis *liquefiant* pondera pennis,

Ignibus emissis, quos mihi nutrit amor?
J: Ducite, Dii! *Phoeben,* rapidis volet ocius alis
Tempus, *at* adducta segnius ire licet.
B: Horas, ah *Corydon!* nunquam prece flectis inani,
Aequali semper labitur hora gradu.
J: O superi, superi, moveat si nostra querela,
Dicite, quid misero nunc medicamen erit?
B: Excute, sanus eris, *Corydon,* fera vincula amoris.
Exulet at talis pectore nympha meo?
J: Haud ita; Dii! charam (semel hoc rogo) ducite *Phoeben,*
Spes prope cum vita destituere meae.
B: Quid faciam? aut miserere, mori aut me denique coges.
Pulchra, mei memores, ora cavete, viri!

J: How easily, o Muses, did I pass the pleasant hours, while the charming Phoebe was with me, a welcome companion!

B: How many (I could scarcely say) and how great were the joys I felt in my heart! Who was ever more happy in his lot than Corydon?

J: Alas! The girl has gone away from here, never to return **(5).** Things have now been darkened and wear a strange appearance.

B: Why has all the beauty of spring perished? Why the glory of the countryside? Ah, now I see! It was she who gave that charm and that splendour.

J: To pasture sheep while beguiling the time by sporting with my girl, or to fall lightly asleep on the sward **(10),**

B: How delightful for me! While the nymph was present to assist me, where was I joyfully transported in my mad love!

J: Now, however, I am sad—how changed, alas, from him! How my vitals swell hot with silent rage!

B: The nymph has gone, and with her has fled my sole pleasure **(15);** My heart! My heavy heart! It cannot bear the weight of its grief.

J: The little stream that used to flow shimmering along its watery channel and to wash its stones with gentle plashes—

B: You know it, Idalian boy! If the nymph just smiled, it pleased these eyes with its course, these ears with its sound **(20).**

J: In her absence, however, while I walk along the edge of the bank, now in hostile mood I utter these reproaches to the deaf waters—

B: "Why do you bound along, merry wave? Why roll these murmurs to my ear? Cease; and do not chatter, water, against my weeping!"

J: While the young lambs frisked around, before their mothers' eyes **(25),** and while she laughed with me at their artless dances,

B: “Quick,” I said, “enjoy your play! These are Saturn’s times!”; now the kindly Cytherean who is the companion of spring, is flourishing.

J: Now, as they go by—”Away with you, be off, you tiresome flock. Be off!” and I throw a handful of grass at their fleeces.

B: Cease, you playful ones! This playfulness makes me sad; you are not in the least touched by my sadness.

J: How fond I was of my faithful *Hylax!* He would often wag his tail and open his mouth to make coaxing woofs.

B: She in delight would say “Come here, my dear little friend”, and with her snowy hand she would gently stroke his head.

J: Now, when he fawns, I reward him with angry words, and he quickly feels a whack from my hard crook.

B: There are further blows in store; when my girl is away, Hylax must not be happy; rather, when I utter sad groans, he must groan too.

J: What sights did I see, ye gods, when my nymph walked with me! What beauty clothed the flowers and fields!

B: On this side shrubs give delight and dark shadows cast by the leaves; on that the crops are smiling and every grove is green.

J: Now the lovely one has gone, and now all the beauty has departed from these things; for me what once was radiant is radiant no longer.

B: For long the deceitful nymph bewitched me with her magic eyes; for long it was an empty image that captured my mind.

J: The woods used to resound to me with their artless song. Nightingale with thrush and lark makes melody.

B: The zephyr’s breath whispered and lambs bleated, while the happy cricket buzzed at my feet.

J: She is gone—the birdsong that previously touched my senses with wondrous sweetness depresses me with gloom.

B: The nymph’s voice (now believe one who has heard it) was like honey; it, above all others, raised a clear song to the stars.

J: Why, o rose, have your petals changed leaving you now pale and withered? Why have the violets lost their purple beauty?

B: Why do the buds wilt and lose their customary scent? Why do the meadows no longer have the same colour as they had before?

J: You were all rivals! You looked brilliant, donning your different colors so that she might wear on her bosom a lovely corsage, though less lovely than herself.

B: You took a delight in pleasing my girl—and it was also a delight to die on her marble breast.

J: How slowly time passes! Come home now, nymph; I am in a fever where the pleasant coolness of the zephyr plays.

B: Where am I to search (for time) so that the weight may melt from his heavy wings by the blasts of fire that are fuelled by my love?
J: Ye gods, bring Phoebe here! Let time fly more swiftly on his rapid wings; but when she is here he may move more sluggishly **(70).**
B: Ah Corydon! your prayer is vain; you can never prevail on the hours. An hour always glides by at the same pace.
J: O heavenly, heavenly powers! If my appeal could move you, tell me, what medicine there will be for me now in my wretchedness?
B: Shake off the cruel fetters of love, Corydon **(75),** and you'll be well. But is such a nymph to be banished from my heart?
J: Not so, ye gods! Bring back my dear Phoebe (I ask just this once). My life has almost faded with my hopes.
B: What shall I do? Either pity me, or you will finally drive me to death. Good fellows, remember my fate, and beware of pretty faces **(80)!**

In revising Walmesley's Latin, Johnson and Stephen Barrett produced a clever but good-natured spoof of a pastoral poem in "amoebaean form," i.e., one in which the first speaker is answered by a second, usually in the same number of lines. The date is 1745; for the occasion of the improvisation see O.429.

In the *Rambler* no. 36, July 21, 1750, which is also available in Wain (1973, 72–75) as well as in the Yale edition, Johnson allowed that "the images of true pastoral have always the power of exciting delight," but he insisted that its range was narrow and incapable of much variety, and that it was not easy to improve on the pastorals of antiquity. In the *Rambler* no. 37, July 24, 1750 (Wain 1975, 76–84) he said it was improper to give the title of a pastoral to verses in which the speakers, after the slight mention of their flocks, fall to complaints of errors in the church, and corruptions in the government, or to lamentations of the death of some illustrious person. This remark anticipates his notorious attack on Milton's *Lycidas* in *Lives of the Poets* (World's Classics, repr. Oxford 1977, vol.1, 112–13). In these contexts Johnson does not mention the innovations made in the genre by Virgil. The present piece is based on the Latin poet's early compositions (in particular no. 3) in which he is closest to Theocritus; it is full of Virgilian motifs and phrases, many of which may be found in B.

19. *Idalium* or *Idalia* was a town in Cyprus sacred to Aphrodite; hence the Idalian boy is Eros/Cupid. **21.** The standard text has "hoc absente," which is clearly wrong, and is shown to be so by the English original printed by B, which has "But now she is absent." **27.** "Saturnia tempora" refer to the golden period when Saturn ruled in Italy. **28.** The Cytherean is Venus. **33.** *Hylax* means "Barker." **57.** The traditional text has the nonsensical "mutatis soliis" (*solium* means a throne). The most convincing emendation (made by Nisbet in correspondence) is *foliis* (petals). The f was mistaken for a long s. **62.** I have removed the standard question mark. This gives better sense and is supported by the original, printed by B.166–68. **63–64.** Barrett's lines hardly reflect the naïve simplicity of the golden age. **67.** The traditional text has *liquefiam;* but *liquefio* is an intransitive verb used as the passive of *liquefacio.* The easiest correction is *liquefiant;* the (leaden) weight of time's wings now becomes the subject. **70.** In view of the strong contrast, *at* (but) is perhaps more likely than the *et* (&) of the standard text.

5
Poems of Doubtful Authenticity

O.445, Y.361, B.172

In Locupletissimum ornatissimumque Syl. Urb. Thesaurum

Menstrua concinnat Sylvanus & annua dona,
  Quantus ubique lepos! quantus ubique decor!
Apte antiqua novis miscentur, et utile dulci:
  Pallas ubique docet; ridet ubique Venus.
Talis in aeterno felix Vertumnus Olympo,
  Mille habet ornatus, mille decenter habet.

On the Most Lavish and Ornate Treasury of Sylvanus Urban

Sylvanus provides monthly and annual gifts. What wit there is everywhere! What charm there is everywhere! Old things are tastefully blended with new, and useful with pleasant. Everywhere is Pallas's teaching; everywhere Venus's humour. Like him is fruitful Vertumnus on everlasting Olympus, as he wears a thousand garbs and wears all thousand becomingly.

These verses, dated 1736, are addressed to Edward Cave, editor of *The Gentleman's Magazine.* Johnson had not yet come to London; so the pseudonym "Rusticus" would have been appropriate. See the poem *Ad Urbanum* (1738).

3. Cf. the Horatian principle: "omne tulit punctum qui miscuit utile dulci" (*Ars Poetica* 343): "He wins every vote who mixes useful with pleasant." **4.** Pallas is Athene, goddess of wisdom, whose Latin equivalent was Minerva. **5–6.** This couplet comes from a piece addressed to the poetess Sulpicia (13–14); it is printed as no. 8 of book 3 in the Tibullan Corpus. The origins of Vertumnus are uncertain, but Johnson (?) is referring to his associations (a) with variety (*verto* = I turn), and (b) with fruitfulness (Ovid describes how he wooed Pomona, the fruit goddess in *Metamorphoses* 14.622ff.; cf. also Propertius 4.2.11–12 and 41–46). So the poet is complimenting Cave on the variety and abundance of his work as a publisher. There is a further link in that a statue of Vertumnus stood in the Vicus Tuscus, the street where Horace's publishers, the Sosii, had their shop (*Epist.*1.20.1–2).

O.445–46, Y.361–62, B.175

On the Gin Act

Pensilibus fusis, cyatho comitata supremo,
  Terribili fremitu stridula moeret anus.
O longum, formosa, vale, mihi vita decusque,
  Fida comes mensae, fida comesque tori!
Eheu! quam longo tecum consumerer aevo!
  Heu! quam tristitiae dulce lenimen eras!
Aeternum direpta mihi! sed quid moror istis?
  Stat: fixum est: nequeunt jam revocare preces.
I, quoniam sic fata vocant: liceat mihi tantum
  Vivere, te viva, te moriente, mori.

The hanging clusters have been all been poured out; with the last beaker as her companion the shrill old crone grieves with terrible shrieks: "O farewell for ever, my lovely, you who were my life and my grace, loyal partner of my bed, loyal partner of my board! Alas! For how long an age would you and I have been drunk together! Alas! How sweet a comfort you were for my sadness! Torn from me for ever! But why do I linger over such thoughts? It is fixed; it cannot be altered. Prayers can no longer bring you back. Go, for this is how the fates are summoning you; may I simply be allowed to live as long as you live, and die when you die."

These verses were signed "Ardelio," an English word for "Meddler"; the Latin was "ardalio." The gin act in 1736 attempted to curb the consumption of gin (a serious social problem) through penal taxation. It proved to be unenforceable, and was watered down in 1743. So in the words of Hanbury-Williams (statesman and poet): "Riot and slaughter once again / Shall their career begin; / And ev'ry parish sucking babe / Again be nurs'd with gin" (a Hogarthian picture). For the ravages of gin see George (1930, 27–43); more recent references are given in B.176.

3. Cf. Virgil, *Eclogues* 3.79 "et longum, formose, vale." **6.** Cf. Horace, speaking to his lyre in *Odes* 1.32.14–15, "o laborum / dulce lenimen." One notes, however, that here the long first *e* of *lenimen* produces a false quantity, a fault which Johnson avoided by using *levamen* in the version of Euripides (O.223). This point casts doubt on the authenticity of the piece. **9.** Cf. Aeneas in his farewell to the young Pallas: "nos . . . fata vocant" (*Aeneid* 11.96–97). These and other classical allusions provide the parodic tone.

O.446, Y.365, B.178

Venus in Armour

Armatam Pallas Venerem conspexit, et "eia
  Nunc age, certamen nunc ineamus," ait;
Dulce Venus ridens, "lorica nil opus," inquit,
  "Vincere te potui nuda; quid arma geram?"

Pallas saw Venus in armour, and said, "Right. Come on now, let us see who wins now." With a sweet smile Venus replied, "I have no need of a breastplate. I managed to beat you when I was naked; why should I wear armor?"

This is a fairly close translation of the *Planudean Anthology* 16.174. Two other Latin versions are attributed to the fourth-century poet Ausonius (see B's note).

2. *Certamen* can mean any contest. The two *nunc*'s are inelegant, but the second might mean "now that we are both armed," in contrast to the occasion recalled by Venus. **3–4.** Venus refers to the beauty contest with Athena and Juno in which Paris awarded her the prize. The question means "Why should I put on armor to compete with you?" But we are left wondering why she should have put on armor at all. Was it just to see how she looked?

O.447, Y. 366, B.181

Ex Cantico Solomonis

Surge, soror dilecta, mihi lux, gaudia, vita;
  Haud mora, surge, soror!

Aspice, diffugiunt ignavae frigora brumae;
Ver geniale venit.
Turbidus imber abest; mittit rosa roscida gemmas,
Sole fovente, suas.
Veris, io! venit alma dies! Philomela canorum
Fundit ab ore melos,
Aeriaeque columbae, dantes oscula, jungunt
Oribus ora suis.
Jam teneros fructus detrudit lactea ficus
Arboreasque comas;
Munera luxurians dat pampinus, et generoso
Subrubet uva mero.
Suaviter exhalant violaria grata, Sabaeo
Spirat odore botrus.
Huc, soror alma, veni! pernicibus ocyor Euris
Huc, soror alma, veni!

From the Song of Solomon

Rise up, dear sister, my light, my joy, my life! Rise up, sister, without delay! Look, the cold of sluggish winter is being dispelled; mild spring is on its way. The stormy rain has gone, the dewy rose is putting forth her buds under the warmth of the sun. Give thanks! The kindly days of spring are coming! Philomela pours out a tuneful song from her throat, the aery doves join bill to bill, exchanging kisses. Now the juicy fig tree is pushing out its soft fruit, and the tresses of its foliage; the luxuriant vine is offering its gifts, and the clusters are dark red, full of noble wine. The lovely violet beds breathe sweet scent, the bunches of grapes send out their Sheban fragrance. Come to me, my dear sister! More quickly than the swift East Wind, dear sister come!

This is a slightly elaborated version of *the Song of Solomon* 2:10–13. The poem is also indebted to Horace, *Odes* 4.7; not only is it written in the same meter (a hexameter followed by the end of a pentameter), which is unique among the odes, it also draws words and phrases from that poem: *diffugiunt, frigora, brumae* (3), *ver* (4), *alma dies* (7), *comas* (12). These Horatian features are quite compatible with Johnson's authorship; for he translated the whole ode in 1784 (O.265). Here, however, he naturally draws only on the joyful half of the poem, omitting the somber conclusion.

1–2. *soror* here and in 17–18 is not in the verses rendered by Johnson—verses which in any case are spoken by the bride. The word comes in 4.9–10 “my sister, my spouse” and again in 5.1. **3.** *ignavae* replaces Horace’s *iners* (4.7.12); for *inertis* would not have fitted in that position in the line. **7.** *Philomela,* the nightingale, is a regular feature of spring poems. **9.** *columbae* destroys the normal caesura after the first syllable of the third foot, and gives the false impression of a hexameter ending. This is not characteristic of Johnson. **12.** *arboreasque comas:* a variation of Horace’s *arboribusque comae* (2). **16.** *botrus* (a Greek word) is not used in classical Latin in the sense of a bunch of grapes.

O.447, Y.366, B.183

The Logical Warehouse: *Occasioned by an Auctioneer’s having the Groundfloor of the Oratory in Lincoln’s-Inn-Fields*

Dissimili domus una duos tenet arte tumentes;
  Praecones ambo, Nummus utrique Deus.
Quaeris, quis prior est fama meritisve; superna
  Cui pars verbosae, vel datur ima, domus?
Supra Praeco Dei, strepit infra Praeco Bonorum:
  Hic bona queis opus est venditat, ille sonum.

A single building houses two windbags of different occupations; both are salesmen, each worships the god of Cash. You ask which is superior in reputation or personal qualities; to which is assigned the upper part and to which the groundfloor of the garrulous building? The salesman of God makes his din upstairs, the salesman of goods makes his below.The latter is trying to sell useful articles; the former merely noise.

The title would be more intelligible if “logical” was a learned joke based on *logos* = “word”; the “wordy warehouse” would then anticipate “verbosae domus” (4); the piece was signed “Philologus.”

2. “Praecones ambo” sounds like a witty distortion of Virgil”s “Arcades ambo’ (*Eclogues* 7.4) in spite of the different meter. Juvenal complains that in Rome wealth is worshipped, even though cash (*nummi*) does not actually have an altar (*Sat.*1.112–14). **5.** Horace speaks of a *praeco* rustling up trade in *Ars Poetica* 419. I do not know how far the swipe at preachers is characteristic of Johnson; cf. Kaminski’s doubts recorded by B.183–84.

O.448, Y.367, B.185

Translation of a Welch Epitaph on Prince Madoc

Inclytus hic haeres magni requiescit Oeni,
Confessus tantum mente manuque patrem;
Servilem tuti cultum contempsit agelli,
Et petiit terras per freta longa novas.

Here rests the famous heir of mighty Owen, taking after his great father in both mind and hand. He scorned the servile cultivation of a safe little plot, and sought a new land across the wide ocean.

The false report of Madoc's discovery of the New World, and its eager acceptance, is set out in *DNB* under Madog ab Owain (1150–80?). This, with the entry under Owain Gwynedd (d. 1169), provides the background to our piece. A late resurgence of the legend (including Madoc's exploits among the Aztecs) is to be found in a formidably lengthy poem by Southey.

O.455, Y.387, B.186

Verses in the Idler

At tu quisquis eris, miseri qui cruda poetae
Credideris fletu funera digna tuo,
Haec postrema tibi sit flendi causa, fluatque
Lenis inoffenso vitaque morsque gradu.

But you, whoever you be, who have thought the untimely death of an unfortunate poet worthy of your tears, may this be the last reason you have for weeping, and may your life and death glide gently on with steady step.

These lines are prefixed to a short essay on grief in the *Idler* no. 41. They are, in effect, a consolation to one mourning the death of a poet. Johnson's mother had died a week before. But in spite of the words "no man who does not hope another year for his parent or friend," there is no specific reference to her. Johnson goes on to say "The life which made my own life pleasant is at an end, and the gates of death are shut upon my prospects." Whatever may be meant by the second sentence, it does not sound like a meditation on his mother; and the next sentence begins "The loss of a friend . . ."

O.457, Y.388, B.189

Translation of Verses by Crashaw

Innocua his membris permistas membra columbas
  Supremis junxit nexibus arctus amor.
Hic jaceant; donec nox transeat horrida nimbis,
  Et cortina novum det revoluta diem!
Tunc alacres demum surgent, et crastinus ortus
  Aeternum aeterna luce juvabit opus!

Here love has closely joined in its final knot two doves that have intertwined harmless limb with limb. Here let them lie, until the rough night with its storms is past, and the curtain, drawn back, lets in the new day. Then at last will they make haste to rise, and tomorrow's dawn will assist with eternal light their eternal occupation.

1. Rather than "doves" we would now probably say "lovebirds." **6.** *opus* must refer to sexual intercourse (*Ox. Lat. Dict.* 1d). The writer has imported this idea into Crashaw's poem (see below); so while Thomas Percy believed that the translation was Johnson's, one may doubt whether this addition is in Johnson's style:

They (sweet Turtles) folded lye
In the last knot that love could tye.
Let them sleepe, let them sleepe on,
Till this stormy night be gone,
And th' eternall morrow dawne.
Then the Curtaines will bee drawne,
And they waken with that Light,
Whose day shall never sleepe in Night.

For the poems of Richard Crashaw see Martin (1927, 174), not the later version on 339–40.

O.457, Y.389, B.190

Epigram on Sir Thomas More, Erasmus, and Micyllus

Τὸ πρῶτον Μῶρος, τὸ δὲ δεύτερον εἶλεν Ἐρασμός,
Τὸ τρίτον ἐκ Μουσῶν στέμμα Μίκυλλος ἔχει.

From the Muses More carried off the first crown and Erasmus the second; Micyllus has the third.

O doubts that this piece was by Johnson, Y thinks it unlikely, B is inclined to accept it. The reader is referred to B's discussion.

Micyllus (Jacob Moltzer, 1503–58) was well known in earlier times as a scholar and poet.

O.458, Y.392, B.195

Verses Wrote on a Window of an Inn at Calais

Eure veni. *Tua* jamdudum exoptata morantur
Flamina; te poscit votis precibusque viator
Impatiens, qui longa morae fastidia sensit.
Interea, ad curvas descendens littoris oras,
Prospicit in patriam, atque avidis exhaurit ocellis,
Nec dulci faciem de littore dimovet unquam:
Illic Dubrenses in coelum assurgere colles
Aspicit, excelsamque arcem, grandesque ruinas,
Et late ingentes scopulorum albescere tractus:
Nequicquam; videt haec, nec fas attingere visa;
Obstat hyems inimica, et vis contraria venti.

Come, East Wind! Your eagerly awaited breezes have long been delayed. The traveller, who has felt the long tedium of delay, calls upon you impatiently with prayers and appeals. Meanwhile, walking down to the curved line of the shore, he looks towards his country, and drinks it in with greedy eyes; and at no point does he remove his gaze from that dear coast. There he sees the crags of Dover rising to the sky, the lofty citadel, and the huge rockfalls, and the mighty expanse of the cliffs gleaming far and wide in their whiteness. All to no avail. He sees these things, and may not reach what he sees; the hostile storm and the power of the adverse wind bar the way.

Y rejects the piece, O is very doubful, but B would like to accept it.

1. The traditional text has *Sua,* but the writer has just addressed Eurus, and in the next line he does so again: "te poscit . . . viator." So *Sua* must be emended to *Tua.* A glance at the facsimile facing p. 98 in Y will show that Johnson's T was sometimes not unlike his S. Nevertheless, I share O's doubts. **8.** The lofty citadel will have been Dover Castle. The *grandes ruinas* could have been the large ruins of buildings, but "huge rockfalls" seems more likely.

B.265

Non Cito Perit Ruinam Qui Primum Timet

Miles, cum telo venienti sibilat aer,
   Elapsus celeri corpore fata fuget;
Sic vigiles oculos intendas undique, vulnus
   Ne *Fortunae* arcu missa sagitta ferat.
Instantem mortem vitasse est gloria major
   Quam nigrum temere precipitasse diem.

He Does Not Soon Die Who Takes Precautions against Destruction

When the air whistles with an approaching javelin, the soldier will escape doom by stealing away with his swift body. So you should keep your eyes open, intent on every side for fear an arrow discharged from Fortune's bow may inflict a wound. It is a greater distinction to avoid the onset of death than, in a moment of rashness, to hasten the arrival of the dark day.

B tells the interesting story of the discovery and provenance of these verses—a story that begins with an article in the *Observer* for January 19, 1992. The text is not very clear, and I have adopted B's suggestion that *fortuna* (?) in line 4 is really *fortunae.* As she owns a bow, I have also given her a capital letter. The rather sardonic realism is not untypical of Johnson, but the phrase "celeri corpore" is not impressive, and Johnson would not have confused *fugo* (2) with *fugio.*

For the sake of completeness I add four lines from *The Gentleman's Magazine* for January 1753, 47. Though not in O or Y, they are printed by B (171–72), who is inclined to attribute them to Johnson.

Ad Atheos

Sic negat esse deos Epicuri de grege porcus:
"Primus in orbe deos fecit ubique timor."
Mentis inops! Primum quid fecit in orbe timorem?
Divorumne timor diis prior esse potest?

The pig from Epicurus's herd denies the existence of the gods thus: "It was fear that first created gods everywhere in the world." Mindless fool! What first created fear in the world? Can the fear of the gods be earlier than the gods?

The echoes of Horace *(Epistles 1.4.16)* in line I and Petronius (Loeb ed. 340) in line 2 are admittedly in Johnson's manner, as is the anti-atheistic stance. But Johnson would have known that in antiquity the Epicureans did believe in the gods, though their divinities were supposed to be indifferent to mankind. Moreover, leaving aside the Epicureans, whether ancient or eighteenth century, one can argue quite consistently from an atheistic position that man invented the gods to explain an often terrifying world, and handed down the doctrine from one generation to another. So it is doubtful if the rather slick sophistry in line 4 should be ascribed to Johnson.

Bibliography

Primary Works

Johnson, Samuel. 1964. *Poems.* Edited by E. L. McAdam, Jr. with George Milne. New Haven.

———. 1974. *The Poems of Samuel Johnson.* 2nd edition. Edited by D. Nichol Smith and E. L. McAdam.

———. 1981. *Johnson's Juvenal: London and The Vanity of Human Wishes.* Edited by Niall Rudd, Bristol.

———. 1982. *The Complete English Poems.* Edited by J. D. Fleeman. New Haven.

———. 1987. *Sixteen Latin Poems,* Edited by Robert L. Barth. Florence, KY.

———. 1991. *Five Latin Poems.* Edited and translated by Thomas Kaminski. Privately printed for the Samuel Johnson Society of the Central Region, Loyola University, Chicago.

———. 1995a. *The Latin and Greek Poems of Samuel Johnson: Text, Translation and Commentary.* Edited by Barry Baldwin. London.

———. 1995b. *Selected Latin Poems.* Edited by Robert L. Barth. Edgewood, KY.

Secondary Works

Bailey, C. 1926. *Epicurus.* Oxford.

Bradner, L. 1940. *Musae Anglicanae: A History of Anglo-Latin Poetry, 1500–1925.* New York.

Brink, C. O. 1982. *Horace on Poetry II. Epistles, Book II.* Cambridge.

Campbell, D. A. 1988. *Greek Lyric Poetry II.* Harvard.

Chapman, R. W. 1961. *A Tour of the Hebrides: Johnson and Boswell.* London.

Clark, J. C. D. 1994. *Samuel Johnson: Religion and English Cultural Politics From the Restoration to Romanticism.* Cambridge.

Clingham, G. 1990. Johnson, Homeric Scholarship, and "The Passes of the Mind." *The Age of Johnson: A Scholarly Annual* 3 (113–70).

Courtney, E. 1993. *The Fragmentary Latin Poets.* Oxford.

Davis, P. M. 1989. *In the Mind of Johnson: A Study of Johnson the Rambler.* London.

Enk, P. J. 1962. *Sex. Propertii Elegiarum Liber Secundus.* Leiden.

Fordyce, C. J. 1961. *Catullus.* Oxford.

Freeman, K. 1956. *Ancilla to the Presocratic Philosophers.* Oxford.

George, M. D. 1930. *London Life in the Eighteenth Century.* London.

Gow, A. S. F., and Page, D. L. 1968. *The Garland of Philip.* 2 vols. Cambridge.

Guthrie, W. K. C. 1962. *A History of Greek Philosophy.* Cambridge.

Greene. D. J. 1977. *Samuel Johnson: Political Writings.* New Haven.

Hill, G. B. and Powell, L. F. (1934–50). *Boswell's Life of Johnson.* 6 vols. Oxford.

Hutton, W. H. 1905. *Burford Papers.* London.

Kaminski, T. 1987. *The Early Career of Samuel Johnson.* New York.

Kramnik, I. 1968. *Bolingbroke and his Circle.* Harvard.

Kupersmith, W. 1970. Declamatory Grandeur: Johnson and Juvenal. *Arion* 9. (52–72).

———. 1972. Juvenal As Sublime Satirist. *PMLA* 87 (508–11).

Lattimore, R. 1962. *Themes in Greek and Latin Epitaphs.* Urbana.

Lovejoy, A. O. and Boas, G. 1997. *Primitivism and Related Ideas in Antiquity.* Baltimore.

Mack, M 1985. *Alexander Pope. A Life.* New Haven.

Martin, L. C. 1927. *The Poems of Richard Crashaw.* Oxford.

Mayor, J. E. B. 1888. *Thirteen Satires of Juvenal.* London.

Money, D. 2002. Samuel Johnson and the Neo-Latin Tradition. In *Samuel Johnson in Historical Context,* edited by J. C. D. Clark and H. Erskine-Hill, 199–221. Basingstoke, Eng.

Nisbet, R. G. M., and Hubbard, M. 1978. *A Commentary on Horace, Odes, Book II.* Oxford.

O'Flaherty, P. 1970. The Rambler's Rebuff to Juvenal: Johnson's Pessimism Reconsidered. *English Studies* 51 (517–27).

O'Sullivan, M. J. 1975. *Ex Alieno Ingenio Poeta:* Johnson's Translation of Pope's Messiah. *Philological Quarterly* 54 (579–91).

Page, D. L. 1981. *Further Greek Epigrams.* Cambridge.

Peterson, R. G. 1975. Samuel Johnson at War with the Classics. *Eighteenth-Century Studies* 9 (69–86).

Raby, F. J. E. 1953. *A History of Christian Latin Poetry.* Oxford.

———. 1957. *A History of Secular Latin Poetry.* 2 vols. Oxford.

Rogers, P. 1996. *The Samuel Johnson Encyclopedia.* Westport, CT.

Rudd, N. 1966. *The Satires of Horace.* Cambridge.

———. 2000. Notes on Johnson's Latin Poetry. *Translation & Literature* 9, no. 2, (215–23).

Selden, R. 1970. Dr Johnson and Juvenal. A Problem in Critical Method. *Comparative Literature* 22 (289–302).

Tucker, S. and Gifford, H. 1957. Johnson's Latin Poetry. *Neophilologus* 41, (215–21).

Venturo, D. 1999. *Johnson the Poet: The Poetic Career of Samuel Johnson.* Newark, DE.

———. 2000. Formal Verse Imitation and the Rhetorical Principles of Imitation in the Neo-Latin Poetry of Samuel Johnson. *SLI: Studies in the Literary Imagination* 33, no. 2, (71–86).

Wain, J. 1973. *Johnson as Critic.* London.

———. 1980. *Samuel Johnson.* London.

Weinbrot, H. 1969. *The Formal Strain: Studies in Augustan Imitation and Satire.* Chicago.

Wiesenthal, A. J. 1979. On the Value of Samuel Johnson's Latin Verse. *Humanistica Lovaniensia: Journal of Neo-Latin Studies* 28, (294–301).

Index of First Lines

Index of Titles

Index of the More Important Proper Names